The Castles of Breconshire

Monuments in the Landscape

Volume VIII

The Castles of Breconshire

by
Paul Remfry

Logaston Press

LOGASTON PRESS
Little Logaston Woonton Almeley
Herefordshire HR3 6QH

First published by Logaston Press 1999
Copyright © Paul Remfry 1999

ISBN 1 873827 80 6

Set in Times 11pt by Logaston Press
and printed in Great Britain by
The Cromwell Press, Wiltshire

Contents

Acknowledgements

I would like to thank all those who, over the years, have aided in the design, writing, checking and publication of this book. Especially I would like to thank all those archaeological and historical friends and acquaintances who have toiled in the libraries and in the field, visiting and recording literary references and visiting all the castles that appear here within. I have enjoyed many happy hours with such a variety of companions in the invigorating search for an understanding of the military actions of our distant forebears. I would particularly wish to thank Brian Byron for drawing the maps and many of the castle plans.

Paul Martin Remfry,
Malvern,
March 1999

Please Note

Some of the monuments mentioned in this book are situated on private land and permission from the owner must, therefore, be obtained before visiting them.

The following points must also be observed:

1. Always follow the Countryside Code.

2. On all sites, extreme care should be taken.

3. Any artefacts found on sites should be reported to the nearest museum.

4. Under no circumstances should visitors dig on or around any site. Any damage could result in prosecution.

5. It is an offence under the 1979 Ancient Monuments and Archaeological Areas Act to use metal detectors on or near scheduled ancient monuments. In addition, simple 'treasure hunting' near ancient monuments can well damage evidence to such an extent that archaeologists are unable to interpret it fully in the future.

The Sources

The history of all the cantrefs and commotes which composed the land of Brecknock in the main castle building age, 1048 to 1285, is generally scant. The bulk of the documentary evidence in this period comes from royal exchequer accounts and monastic chronicles. The royal records consist firstly of the pipe rolls and later the close, patent, fine, curia regis and charter rolls. The pipe rolls, or great roll of the pipe, were great parchments about $2^1/_2$ feet wide and between 4 and 10 feet long. These 'membranes' were then bound together at the top into leaves and rolled up and stored in a pipe, hence their name. On both sides of the membrane, Exchequer accounts would be kept of how monies had been expended and collected in each shire, or sometimes by barony depending on whether there was a royal interest in the fief. These accounts were drawn up at Michaelmas each year and covered the previous twelve months. Like all numerical systems the pipe rolls were not infallible and mistakes often occur in the calculations, and the amounts owed sometimes do not tally either individually or from year to year. At other times cryptic comments are placed in the texts. Often no pipe roll was produced for the counties bordering the Marches due to the disturbed state of the country. Brecknock, as Marcher land, rarely appeared in the great roll of the pipe as its administration as a border region was exempt from royal interference. However, when a lord of Breconshire died or rebelled, royal ministers were often sent into the land to administer it and often they returned interesting accounts of the land and its tenants. The pipe rolls may have originated in the reign of William Rufus (1087-1100) but our first survivor is the 31st roll (1130) of Henry I's reign (1100-35). The series was kept through the turbulence of Stephen's reign, but unfortunately none of his have survived until Henry II (1154-89) joined him in governing the kingdom in 1154. From here on the series is nearly complete and is a useful source for the dates of the succession to a barony and the financial viability of its holder.

The close and patent records are very similar, being royal instructions or mandates issued to barons, officials or foreigners recorded in rolls. In other words they are a complete list of royal correspondence, close documents being sealed and intended only for those people as addressees, and patent documents being open for all to see and know. Fine rolls were simply a list of monies owed to the Exchequer, often closely dated and giving invaluable information on the dates of succession to baronies. The curia regis rolls were records of court cases brought before the king's court. These carry many interesting stories of how daily life was run, and often interrupted, in the Middle Ages. Finally come the charter rolls. These were in many ways the most important of the rolls. They consisted of written instruments telling of land holdings and who had granted what to whom and often when. Importantly they were also witnessed and the witness lists on these charters often tell who was associating with whom, where and occasionally exactly when. Such information is often invaluable in unravelling the veiled history of a barony. All these rolls are tolerably complete from the commencement of the reign of King John (1199-1216), who was responsible for their inauguration.

There are few non-royal transactions or documents of use in unravelling the history of Breconshire. Most of these are land grants to the priory of Brecon founded by Bernard Neufmarché. These charters are preserved in what is called a cartulary—a Medieval list of charters kept for easy reference and proving the cartulary holder's rights to their lands. In many ways these are simply provincial and often more detailed versions of the royal charter rolls. Our only ancient knowledge of these Brecon documents comes from a late copy of about 1710, made by a scribe who knew little of 13th century handwriting. Therefore some of the readings are suspect, but is nevertheless a source of the highest importance for Breconshire.

The Welsh Chronicles sketch in barest outline some of the recorded history though, as with Radnorshire, they are not really interested in this region except when the princely stock of the

Chroniclers' regions became involved in the affairs of the Marches. That said, they provide the bones of the chronology on which the flesh of our story must be hung.

Of great help in distinguishing the various Welsh characters who regularly appear in various documents are the later genealogies in the British Museum and the National Library of Wales. Most of these genealogical sources have been compiled by P.C. Bartrum, but as he himself notes, these mainly 15th century works cannot be regarded as one hundred per cent accurate.

Giraldus Cambrensis is a source of the greatest importance when supplying specific detail on the affairs of Brecknock which would otherwise have stood little chance of having been preserved. Giraldus' views are especially interesting as he spent much of the middle years of his life at Llanddew Castle, just north-east of Brecon, where there had long been a residence for the Archdeacon of Brecon.

Ordericus Vitalis is also of great value for the earliest periods of the Norman Conquest, but it must be remembered that Oderic was writing from Normandy about his homeland around Shrewsbury, which he had left when young.

Some caution must also be shown in making use of the various monastic chronicles from which much information is drawn, as most commence as compilations, copies, or worse. The best of these concerning the Middle March is undoubtedly the so-called chronicle of Benedict of Peterborough, which was compiled roughly contemporaneously with the events it describes, and was apparently copied in part by Roger of Hoveden. Information additional to these chronicles can be drawn from the poetry of the era, but this must be recognized as an extremely hazardous source.

Sources for the later part of the work are mainly derived from Professor R.R. Davies, *The Revolt of Owain Glyn Dwr* (Oxford, 1995) and Hodges, G., *Owain Glyn Dwr & the War of Independence in the Welsh Borders* (Logaston, 1995), both of whom have trawled the available records for these periods as I have for the earlier, castle-building time of 1070 to 1282.

Apart from the historical sources there is one other source to be drawn upon—the archaeological evidence. In Breconshire this manifests itself, as elsewhere, pre-eminently in the advance of the castle.

When time permits many works are planned dealing with individual Breconshire castles and their history. The monograph for Hay-on-Wye Castle has already been published and those for Castell Dinas and Brecon are under construction. Such works contain full bibliographical references. This and other booklets on castles and Anglo-Norman History are available direct from SCS Publishing, 31 Richmond Road, Malvern Link, Worcs, WR14 1NE. Tel: 01684 572224.

The History of
Breconshire's Castles

Introduction

The county of Breconshire was formed in 1536 when Henry VIII abolished the Marcher Lordships of Wales and created counties in their wake. In 1974 the 733 square mile shire was included in the larger land unit of Powys.

Castles were built when Breconshire consisted of the remnants of several Welsh land units called cantrefs and their sub-divisions known as commotes. These lands had by and large been conquered in the late 11th century and welded into two Norman lordships—the larger one to the south was Brecknock, (now more commonly referred to as Brecon, but itself a corruption of the name of the older Welsh kingdom of Brycheiniog), whilst to the north the lordship of Builth was formed from the old Welsh cantref of Buellt.

Late in 1165 the lordship of Brecon was inherited by the Norman lord of Builth and the two land units were amalgamated, a process disrupted by the death in 1230 of the last Braose lord of both districts. The two lordships once more diverged and it was not until 1536 that they were permanently united. Unlike neighbouring Radnorshire the Norman conquest of Brecon proved reasonably permanent, although Prince Llywelyn ap Gruffydd occupied most of the district between 1263 and 1274. This brief interruption did little to arrest the Anglicization of the southern part of the shire, a process not noticeable to the north in Buellt where the old Welsh commotes are still tolerably traceable. In the southern Brecon Lordship the Norman assimilation swept away all real trace of these old land units and their boundaries. In their place, especially in the east of the barony, the Norman lordships of Hay, Glasbury, Talgarth, Crickhowell, Tretower, Pencelli, Blaenllyfni, Melinog and Llansantffraed or Scethrog were formed. In the Middle Ages the two western parts of southern Breconshire were called Cantref Mawr and Cantref Selyf, possibly indicating some memory of the older Welsh land units.

In the east of Breconshire there is also evidence of earlier Saxon penetration. The land of Glasbury seems to have been under Saxon control from an early period and its etymology may suggest a Saxon origin rather than a Welsh 'clas' foundation. The names in the 'commote' of Talgarth also suggest Saxon penetration of this region. The ancient Irish capital of the kingdom of Brycheiniog had for many centuries lain in Llangorse or Mara Lake just south of the town. Unlike the rest of Breconshire the Llangorse region is full of Welsh 'Trefs', or townships, but associated with some very English sounding names such as Tregunter and Tredustan as well as the more Norman sounding Trephilip, Trewalkin and Trewalter. There are also the more Welsh sounding Tredurn, Tredomen, Trefeca and Trefeinion. Nowhere else in the county is there such a cluster of 'Trefs'.

The distribution of castles across Breconshire is uneven, for geographical as much as for political reasons. Few castles existed in the more forbidding mountains and wastes of the west and south, where the population was probably less dense and more itinerant. The major routes run east to west, the main route now being followed by the A40 which bisects the county from Abergavenny to Llandovery, whilst the A470 runs from Hereford to Brecon. It is along these ancient routes that many of the castles are positioned.

Of the total of 50 castle sites, only 18 are mentioned in historical sources between 1066 and 1536. The chief castles of the Norman lordships are most frequently mentioned — Brecon, Builth Wells, Pencelli, Blaenllyfni, Tretower, Crickhowell, Bronllys and Hay-on-Wye, while the history of their supporting castles has to be largely surmised. Doubtless castles fell and were retaken without record, but events concerning those of strategic importance such as

Map showing the location of castles within Breconshire

the chief castle of a commote or lordship are likely to find mention in contemporary records, especially from the mid-12th century onwards.

The archaeological evidence provides information about changes in castle design, demonstrating that even apparently simple sites often have more than one phase of building. It is difficult to relate these phases to the terse entries of castle building and destruction in the various documents, partly because castle design varied over the years, and individual sites were also unsystematically altered as new military innovations occurred. Added to the complex structural remnants of these fortresses are the problems of accurate dating and even of assessing what the visible remains represent.

The main purpose of the castle was military, accommodation on the frontier being of secondary interest to self-preservation. The castle provided a secure base whilst military forces were built up to destroy any attackers—in the Middle Ages most battles were clashes between besiegers and those attempting to relieve the besieged. It was only later, following pacification, that the castle was abandoned for new, cheaper and more homelike surroundings. Thus there is often a manor house or farm adjacent to a castle ruin, but the old castle was still there just in case, a kind of insurance policy. This is superbly illustrated by Tretower Castle and Court which stand adjacent to each other.

Life was relatively cheap in the Medieval era and many disputes were settled by violence rather than the law. Even those that did reach the courts often refer to previous use of violence. Thus, in 1248, William Valance of Pembroke appeared in the royal court against William Theobald, Humphrey Bohun's bailiff of Haverford and St Clears, demanding why he had entered his liberty of Pembroke, wounded his men, imprisoned others in Haverfordwest Castle and killed a horse to the value of 40 marks? Similarly, on 14 May 1256, Fulk fitz Warin of Whittington complained that John Fitz Alan of Oswestry had broken and destroyed his parks, plundered and burned his lands, and taken and imprisoned his kinsmen. Such relatively petty disputes characterise the warlike side of Marcher life. On the other side is that irrepressible spirit seen so often in troubled border areas, a self reliance and dislike of all things alien. This was the land of the Welsh Princes and Marchers, both of whom fought for their own liberty and independence against the Crown as well as against each other.

In this constantly disturbed landscape the castle was a durable sign of authority. In December 1256 Prince Llywelyn overran the cantref of Buellt, but could not take Builth Wells Castle. By Easter 1257, the castle garrison had brought the local Welsh back to their fealty to the Crown. In January 1259 Llywelyn returned and again occupied the land but not the castle. By 10 April Roger Mortimer of Wigmore had brought the cantref back to royal obedience and was sending 'malefactors' to Bridgnorth Castle for incarceration at the royal will. Once again the power of the castle to overawe a district was made plain. In January 1260 Llywelyn yet again invaded the cantref and this time besieged the castle with siege engines. Even so, Roger Mortimer managed to raise the siege and by April had brought the province back under English control once more. From this the personal element of rule can also clearly be seen. In the absence of a prime military leader in the district, at least one whose orders would be backed by force, nothing seems to have been done.

The dispute over Buellt was ended on 17 July 1260, when Roger Mortimer was in London. That night Builth Wells Castle was treacherously surrendered to the local Welsh, and subsequently Rhys Fychan of Dinefwr demolished the castle so thoroughly that English rule ended in the district until 1276. Without the castle to dominate the land the task of subduing the district was considered too difficult and the cantref was abandoned as uneconomic until times had become more favourable for the invaders to re-assert their authority, rebuild the castle and dominate the district.

In the early days lords were itinerant, moving from place to place with their increasingly large retinues. A lord could not stay for long in one place because of the cost to the local community—he would literally eat them out of house and home. In 1278, when Prince Llywelyn ap Gruffydd was in dispute with the Abbot of Basingwerk, he expected the abbot to entertain his retinue of 500 men at a cost of some £8 over the year. This was a large sum when the average foot soldier only received 2d. a day, an annual wage of just over £3 a year. Manual labourers may have only earned half that amount.

But there was another reason why the lord had to be itinerant. Loyalty, especially in the early days, was strictly personal and if the lord did not show his face to his vassals often enough they could turn to another for protection and advancement. This was a particular problem in the Marches where often several barons, both Norman and Welsh, claimed the same piece of land. Consequently, peasants could find life totally unbearable, being taxed by both sides to support the wars that were fought over the lands they were trying to farm. Consequently, loyalty in the Marches proved fickle. In some histories it is suggested that the tenants proved turncoats in their allegiance, but most had no 'deep' allegiance—they would support the lord who was the most powerful at the time rather than risk losing all in, what was to them, the vagaries of political warfare. Whilst the tenants looked to their lord for protection, the lord considered his peasants as a source of income. If a village proved reluctant to obey him, it was far better to destroy it and suffer the loss rather than have the disobedience spread and lose all of his tenants to another lord.

When the lord was not in residence in his castle, it was in the care of a constable and one or two paid soldiers. In times of war, the garrison would rapidly be augmented by the local populace and landholders who owed military service to their lord for the privilege of holding their lands. As it was impossible to move a large attacking force quickly, a castle garrison usually had time to form its defence. Generally the feudal military land obligation was a period of service at the tenant's own cost, sometimes in person, sometimes by a certain number of knights, mounted infantry, bowmen or footmen, for a set number of days. Initially the service was for 40 days and the knights were accommodated in their own houses in the castle, but as these fees, as they were called, were split amongst co-heirs the amount of service would diminish and by the 13th century many obligations were down to just a few days. For a lord wishing to undertake military operations such a piecemeal and part-time army was obviously less than satisfactory, and so military obligations tended to be replaced by a cash payment, generally known as scutage or shield money which enabled a lord to hire professional armed forces.

The lords of individual castles also tended to owe military service for their lands to a greater lord. Thus, around 1165 William

Braose on inheriting Brecon lordship confirmed Glasbury Castle and Cantref Selyf to Walter Clifford on condition that he continued to supply 40 days military service with 5 knights at Brecon Castle in time of war, together with an annual render of a sparrowhawk. Braose, no doubt like his predecessors, also reserved to himself all judgements in matters affecting life and limb over the men of Glasbury lordship. Similar obligations and responsibilities were no doubt also owed from the lords of Hay-on-Wye, Tretower, Bronllys, Pencelli and Crickhowell.

Castle building in Breconshire occurred in phases. The greatest number were built after the initial Norman assault and colonisation of Brecknock in the period 1048 to 1099. These were mainly of the motte and bailey type—a large steep-sided conical mound with a defensive enclosure at its base. Then came a period of military stagnation which lasted until 1231, the exception being some castle building in the cantref of Buellt and the 'commote' of Talgarth in the early 13th century. After 1231 many castles were stormed and burnt by the Welsh under Llywelyn Fawr, but few seem to have been occupied by him. This led to substantial rebuilding of castles, often in stone, with new elements of design reflecting new military needs. Warfare continued intermittently for the next 50 years until Prince Llywelyn ap Gruffydd was killed in the cantref of Buellt in December 1282. After this the need for castles in Breconshire lessened and many began to be converted into more luxurious accommodation. Others, like Tretower, were superseded by new country houses.

The revolt of Owain Glyndwr in the early 1400s led to many castles being patched up and several sieges resulted, though few if any castles seem to have actually fallen. After this, many castles were dismantled or left to quietly decay. Builth Wells Castle was used for building stone after the town burned down in the reign of Elizabeth I. By the time of the Civil War no castles in the county were seriously defensible. Indeed the county seems to have taken up a position of armed neutrality, although willing to provide Charles I with supplies of men and materials. When the end came in 1645, the townsmen quickly dismantled the ancient and now indefensible ruins of Brecon Castle so that no resistance could be offered to the victorious parliament.

Tretower Castle

The Castles

Castle building in Breconshire followed a pattern similar to that in the rest of the borders and Wales. A castle was first built at the centre of a new lordship, or old commote. This major fortress was then surrounded by smaller fortresses, built by the knights who held land and owed military service at the major castle. Aberyscir, Cilwhybert, Llandefaelog-Fach, Alexanderstone and Castell Madog may be the five early castles of Brecon Lordship, surrounding the late 11th century castle.

The positioning of castles in the landscape was always of crucial importance, and once chosen, the site was rarely changed. Whilst royal castles were generally built as administrative centres or to overawe a settlement, the major barons built their principal fortresses both for comfort and show. Against this the frontier castles were merely constructed for strategic purposes, guarding exposed vills and as outposts for the adventurers in these dangerous lands.

Some of the castles in Wales must have been constructed in stone from their inception, Chepstow, probably Monmouth, and apparently Degannwy being the earliest. Others were only ever built in timber: Hen Domen, Montgomery, the major castle of a small Marcher Barony, despite being fortified at the end of the 13th century, had no stonework.

Along the Vale of Usk in central Brecknock there are some 11 castles of which nine certainly contained stone components: Trecastle, Sennybridge, Aberyscir, Brecon, Pencelli, Scethrog Tower, Maescelyn, Crickhowell and Llangadock. Of these only Sennybridge and possibly Crickhowell and Scethrog Tower seem to be 13th century foundations, the rest being 12th century or earlier. The eviction of the garrisons from these sites proved next to impossible for the local Welsh, as was seen in the campaigns of 1093, 1096, 1135-6, 1168, 1231, 1233, 1262 and 1265. Castles which did fall seem mainly to have been victims of either a surprise attack, treachery, or due to the collapse of Norman will to hold down a district. In the latter case, this tended to lead to the granting of castles to members of the local princely stock in exchange for their support in English politics!

There was a remarkable change in the theory of fortification in Wales and the March in the early 13th century. At this date motte and baileys were still being built, two new ones apparently being constructed (or reconstructed) at Builth Wells in 1210 and Mathrafal in 1212. These could have been the last mottes built in Britain. In their place, during the reign of Henry III, impressive stone citadels were built on great crags, possibly in the Poitou style. Thus in 1223, a new castle was founded at Montgomery on an elevated position, and a new rock fortress at Beeston was begun around 1225. In the Marches new castles in this mould appeared at Cefnllys, Knucklas and Tinboeth in neighbouring Radnorshire, but none appear further south in Bohun held Breconshire. This might be because the lordship of Brecon was never re-conquered by the Welsh with the exception of the short term conquest by Llywelyn ap Gruffydd in 1262-73.

Pre-Norman Breconshire, Commotes and Cantrefs

Before the Norman Conquest Breconshire was divided into cantrefs, the approximate equivalents of English hundreds. Each

CWMWD
DEUDWR

GWRTHEYRNION

CARDIGAN-
SHIRE

Llydsdinam

Llanafan-fawr ●

ELFAEL

Forest Twdin ●

Caerau ●

Caer Beris

Builth Wells

BUELLT

CARMARTHEN-
SHIRE

Crickadarn II (or Waun Gunllwch) ●

Crickadarn I

GLASBURY

Hay-on-Wye

CANTREF SELYF

Llyswen ●

Llanigon

Clawdd British ●

Castle Madog ●

Aberllynfi

HAY

Llandefaelog-Fach

Tredustan

Bronllys

Talgarth

Trefecca

TALGARTH

Trecastle ●

BRECON

Llanddew

Alexanderstone

Trefecca fawr

Aberyscir

Ty'-y-Caeau

Castell Dinas

Sennybridge ●

Pont Estyll

Garn y Castell

EWIAS

Cwm Camlais ●

Cilwhybert ●

Pencelli

Twmpan
Scethrog

Blaenllyfni

CANTREF
MAWR

TIR
RALPH
or
PENKELLY

YSTRAD
YW

Tretower

Maescelyn

Crickhowell

Hen Castell

Ystradfellte ●

Vaynor

CRICKHOWELL

GLAMORGAN

GWENT

*Map showing the Cantrefs of Breconshire,
together with adjoining terirtories*

cantref was subdivided into three or four commotes—the smallest units of justice. In England service was owed to the Hundred Court, in Wales it was owed to the commotal court or llys. Consequently, when the Normans invaded Wales, they used the commote as the unit of penetration in a manner similar to the way they had absorbed England. In Wales the lord of a commote was a man of great importance and was apparently called a king, even though he may have owed allegiance to his neighbours who were more powerful. The situation has been rightly compared to a crazy jigsaw puzzle of interlocking and overlapping spheres of influence, each a kingdom in its own right. This was anathema to the orderly-minded feudal barons of Normandy.

The early kingdom of Brycheiniog is said to have been divided into three cantrefs, Cantref Selyf—the cantref of Solomon, Cantref Tewdos—the cantref of Theodosius, and Cantref Einion which later became Talgarth. These three men, Solomon, Theodosius and Einion, were said to have been the sons of one Einion ap Gruffydd ab Elise, who may have been descended from Irish adventurers. This division, if it ever occurred, took place in the 9th century. In 848 the men of Brycheiniog, probably led by their king or kings, slew King Iudhail of Gwent. By the 880s the only remaining king of Brycheiniog, Elisedd, had paid homage to King Alfred and it is to be presumed that he felt it expedient to ask for English help in the running of his realm. Such an alliance may well have been due to Viking pressure, for in the spring of 896 Brycheiniog, Gwent and Gwynllwg were devastated by the Norsemen who had wintered that year at Quatford near Bridgnorth. According to the monk Asser, another reason for Elisedd seeking the protection of King Alfred was that his realm was being brought under pressure from an expansionist Gwynedd.

In the early summer of 916 Brycheiniog faced a greater menace when Aethelflaed, the daughter of King Alfred and wife of the Earl of Mercia, invaded. On 19 June the royal llys in *Brecenan Mere*, which can only be the crannog in Llangorse Lake, was stormed and the queen and 34 others were captured. It is probable that Tewdwr ab Elisedd was king at the time for he was at the English royal court in 934 where he witnessed a charter. After Tewdwr no more kings of Brycheiniog are recorded and all that can be said of

11

King Gwrgant ap Bleddyn of Brycheiniog, who is claimed to have been defeated by Bernard Neufmarché in 1093, is that he seems to exist nowhere other than in the fanciful imagination of much later antiquarians.

By 983 the kings of Brycheiniog had been replaced by the kings of Deheubarth, and Brecknock formed part of the extensive possessions of Einion ab Owain, the grandson of Hywel Dda, when the land was ravaged by Hywel ap Iueaf and Aelfhere, leader of the English. Einion counter-attacked this force, inflicting heavy losses and then pushed on into Gwent where he was slain either this year or in 984. In 991, his brother, Maredudd, attacked Maes Hyfraid (Radnor), probably from his base of Brycheiniog. At that time Radnor was held by the English for in the following year they replied, with the help of Owain ab Einion, by harrying Maredudd's territories in Deheubarth. The events of 992 may have weakened Maredudd, for in 994 he was attacked by Meurig of Gwynedd and his sons and defeated at a battle near Langwm, Pembrokeshire, where Tewdwr ab Einion seems to have been killed. With King Gruffydd ap Llywelyn, a contemporary of Edward the Confessor (1042 to 1066), Wales and Brycheiniog reached the age of castles.

The Norman arrival in Wales

Little has been recorded of the Normans' early thrusts into Wales so our knowledge of Breconshire is much buttressed by occurrences elsewhere and by what is recorded in the Domesday Book.

King Edward the Confessor was himself raised in the Norman way of life. Consequently when he succeeded to the English throne he brought some of his youthful friends over from Normandy. In the period after 1048 some of these men were placed in exposed lands in Herefordshire where King Gruffydd was causing problems. According to the English chronicles, by 1051 'the foreigners [Normans] had built a castle in Herefordshire in Earl Swein's province and had inflicted every possible insult and injury upon the king's men in those parts.'

After 1052 at the latest, Hereford gained a Norman earl in the form of King Edward's nephew, Ralph Mantes. Other Normans in the district included Richard fitz Scrope of latterday Richard's Castle, Robert fitz Wymarch of Thruxton, and Osbern Pentecost. A little later Earl Ralph's son, Harold, was to obtain part of this land and give to it its lasting name of Ewias Harold.

In 1055 King Gruffydd marched on Hereford to defeat its earl in battle on 24 October, and destroy the town and castle. This slight to Herefordshire was rapidly repaid by Earl Harold Godwinson. The two men came to terms in February 1056. The matter of the desecration of Hereford Cathedral in 1055 was not, however, allowed to rest. In March 1057 one Leonegar was elected bishop of Hereford. He immediately set out with an army to deal with his Welsh enemy, marching up the Wye valley to Glasbury in Breconshire where he was slain together with his clergy, the sheriff Agelnoth, and many others by King Gruffydd. He had enjoyed his bishopric for only 11 weeks and 4 days.

Soon after the coronation of William the Conqueror at Christmas 1066 the king granted vast power to his distant relation and friend, William fitz Osbern. Among the many honours poured upon William was the earldom of Hereford together with many rights in the neighbouring counties of Worcestershire and Gloucestershire. Walter Lacy of Lassy, Calvados, was also established, probably by the Conqueror, in Herefordshire and elsewhere as an ally, but not a subject, of Earl William. In Domesday the fore-runner of the Lacy honour of Longtown was recorded as 'a land called Ewias within the land of Ewias' held by Walter's son, Roger Lacy. It did not belong to the castlery (Ewias Harold) nor to the hundred (Cutsthorn). This is a classic description of a Marcher barony, self contained in the administration of its own affairs, distinct from royal administration and yet a part of the kingdom of England.

It was William fitz Osbern who probably made the first Norman attempt to hold sway over the greater part of Breconshire. In 1068 and 1069 severe fighting against an alliance of the Saxons and Welsh took place along the northern half of the Welsh border, forcing Earl William to relieve the besieged Norman garrison of Shrewsbury in the desperate campaign of 1069. The following year the earl was able to turn his attention against the Welsh who had aided the rebellious Saxons, and in the summer he defeated three Welsh kings in Brycheiniog. These kings were recorded by Ordericus Vitalis, writing from Normandy about his homeland around Shrewsbury, as Maredudd, Rhys, and Cadwgan.

Maredudd was Maredudd ab Owain, and Rhys was his brother; they were successively kings of Deheubarth or south Wales. The third is likely to be King Cadwgan ap Meurig who was said, in a charter preserved by the bishop of Llandaff, to have ruled Glamorgan 'as far as the wooden way over the Tywi' as well as Ystrad Yw, Gwent Uwch Coed and Gwynllwg during the time of Earl William of Hereford. Cadwgan was a direct descendant of Hywel Dda and was therefore a claimant to hegemony not only in Deheubarth, but in Wales as a whole. However, his power seems to have failed with him, for he left no political heirs and is last heard of with certainty some time before 1075 when he was at least partially succeeded by King Rhydderch. The fact that Cadwgan and Rhydderch were said to have been subservient to King William implies that this was the Cadwgan defeated by fitz Osbern in the summer of 1070, rather than the Cadwgan ab Elystan Glodrydd of central Wales.

Maredudd ab Owain had been king of Deheubarth since 1069 and would obviously have opposed any incursion by William fitz Osbern into central and southern Wales. He was killed in battle on the River Rhymni near Cardiff in 1072 by King Caradog ap Gruffydd together with his Norman crossbowmen. That Caradog was engaging his enemy with Norman soldiers—the *Annales Cambriae* states simply that the French killed Maredudd—suggests that Caradog was using the soldiers of Earl Roger of Hereford, the second son and successor of Earl William fitz Osbern who had invaded Brycheiniog just two years earlier.

In 1081 Caradog, despite his early advantage and Norman support, was defeated. It was probably at this time that Norman troops occupied Ystrad Yw and castles were begun in the valley of the Usk above Abergavenny, although it is also possible that the fortresses had already been commenced under Caradog's auspices and that the Norman Picards and Turbevilles were part of the forces that had followed Caradog into his later battles.

Bernard Neufmarché and the Norman assault of 1093

What exactly happened in Breconshire after the failed rebellion of Earl Roger of Hereford in 1075 is uncertain. Contemporary accounts state that Earl Roger raised large numbers of Welshmen and it can be presumed that many came from Brycheiniog, Gwent and Cynllibiwg, areas over which Earl Roger had at least gained partial control. The defeat of the earl allowed the king to extinguish the earldom of Hereford and in its place appoint his own officials. Within the old earldom, the king elevated nobles from mere tenants of the earl to tenants in chief, holding their lands directly from the Crown. Into this category to some degree fit such barons as the Neufmarchés, Gloucesters, Mortimers and Tosnys.

It was thought that Bernard Neufmarché first came to prominence in 1070/1 when he witnessed a charter of William the Conqueror, but this and another charter of 1074-78 have now been dismissed as forgeries. Consequently the first reliable reference to Bernard occurs in 1079 when, according to Ordericus Vitalis, he exchanged land for the two Herefordshire churches of Brinsop and Burghill.

When Bernard joined the Marcher rebellion against King William Rufus at Easter 1088, several chroniclers recorded Bernard as the son-in-law of Osbern fitz Richard fitz Scrope, the lord of Richard's Castle. Indeed, charters indicate that Bernard had at some point been granted by Osbern part of Bodenham, Little Hereford and Berrington in the Teme valley, together with his daughter for wife (whom Odericus informs us was called Agnes). This must have occurred after Domesday, when those lands were recorded as still belonging to Osbern.

Before his rebellion in March 1088 Bernard had made a charter in favour of Gloucester Abbey during the time of Bishop Serlon (1072-1104). By this charter Bernard granted to the monks the land of Glasbury and its church of St Kenedri with all the tithes of his lordship in Brycheiniog which included grain, cattle, cheese, game and honey together with lands in Cowarne in Herefordshire. Such a grant would indicate that Bernard's penetration of Brycheiniog was more than just superficial. Traditionally this document is dated to 1088 as a later writer has written this date by the charter. Obviously this 'evidence' is next to worthless, though we can see from where the interpolator based his guess. Following the two slightly different versions of Bernard's original grant is a confirmation charter by none other than William Rufus himself. This carries a dating clause that the confirmation was made in the year when war raged amongst the leaders of England and when Gloucester and the church of St Peter were destroyed. This we know from other sources refers to the rebellion of Easter 1088. If the king did confirm the charter of Bernard Neufmarché after putting down the rebellion of his Marchers, as would seem a logical thing to do, then all that can be said of Bernard's grant is that it was made between 1075 and 1088 and that any date in this period is equally possible.

By the spring of 1093 Bernard Neufmarché's encroachment into Brecknock had progressed to the extent that he was building a castle at Brecon, a castle that was to prove pivotal for the Norman Conquest of Wales. King Rhys ap Tewdwr of Deheubarth moved against Bernard with an army. Not very much is known of the resulting battle, except that it was decisive (the Welsh Chronicles carry the poignant statement that: 'From that day forth [in Easter week, 17-23 April] kings ceased to rule in Wales'), and that it seems to have taken place north of Brecon. The name of the little village of Battle two miles north of the town may be indicative of the site, or merely the fact that Bernard founded a priory at Brecon which he granted to Battle Abbey in Sussex, and which included this district.

Battle Abbey had been founded by William the Conqueror on the site of his victory over King Harold II at Hastings 27 years before, and by his gesture Bernard seems to offer thanks for a similar great victory over a powerful enemy. As no foundation charter for the priory exists, the only source of information is Ordericus Vitalis, who says that Bernard held the old kingdom for many years before he made Brecon 'the chief castle' of the lordship, lending credence to Bernard's possible activities in Brycheiniog over a number of years.

The battle of Brecon brought about a decisive change in Welsh politics. First the Welsh of Powys tried to capitalise on the catastrophic defeat of the royal forces of Deheubarth by attempting to annexe Ceredigion, and then the Normans struck from several directions and the remaining kings of Wales found themselves utterly incapable of protecting their homelands. Drogo fitz Pons, the under-tenant of the Tosnys of Clifford in Herefordshire, founded a new castle at Llandovery next to Bernard Neufmarché's land of Brecon. To the north, Ralph Tosny of Clifford Castle invaded the Welsh cantref of Elfael and built a castle at Colwyn.

The Baskervilles, tenants of Bernard Neufmarché, appear to have set up their own independent barony at Aberedw on the Wye in Radnorshire and also gained lands at Pilleth in Radnorshire, at Pencelli and south of Talgarth at Trewalter in Breconshire. The Baskerville family seems to have hailed from Bacqueville some 10 miles south-east of Rouen, near to the family homes of the Marcher families of Pitres, Mucegros and Tosny. Robert Baskerville is noted as a landholder in Herefordshire in Domesday Book, and is known to have still been alive in 1109 when he returned from Jerusalem and granted some of his Gloucestershire lands to Gloucester Abbey. He was probably the first mesne lord of Pencelli and the founder of Pencelli Castle.

William Braose (1063-c.1094), or more likely his son Philip (1073-c.1138), invaded the northern Breconshire cantref of Buellt during this time and built a castle to control the commote. The village which grew up around the castle was later to become the important market town of Builth Wells. It has been generally accepted that the later Edwardian castle was built on the site of Braose's castle, but it is perhaps more likely that the motte and bailey at the west end of Builth, at Caer Beris, was the first castle in the district. Indeed, even its name seems suggestive, apparently being a corruption of Caer Braose, the fortress of Braose. The act of conquest had probably occurred by 11 December 1093, when both William and Philip Braose were back in Normandy.

Further north, the Mortimers of Wigmore moved into central Wales and founded a castle at Dinieithon, the caput of their lordship of Maelienydd. Mortimer and Baskerville forces also penetrated as far as Aberystwyth where the earl of Shrewsbury founded or re-founded a castle to aid him in his conquest of Ceredigion. The furthest extent of the Norman push took the earl's brother, Arnulf, to Pembroke where another great Norman castle was founded. All Wales had now fallen under the direct sway of the invader, no more were native client kings to be allowed to rule in the name of the kings of England. Well might the Worcester chronicler write that with Rhys 'the kingdom of the Welsh fell', whilst the *Welsh Annals* recorded that in the newly conquered lands of central and south Wales the Normans 'built castles there and occupied all the lands of the British.'

The Welsh Backlash, 1094-99

This great invasion of Wales brought about an inevitable backlash. In 1094 the Welsh of north Wales rose in rebellion, followed by those of Ceredigion and Deheubarth. The following year William Rufus was active in Gwynedd, whilst forces, probably from Glamorgan and Breconshire, seem to have moved into Gower, Kidwelly and Ystrad Tywi, devastating the land.

The year 1096 opened ominously for the Normans. William fitz Baldwin, the castellan of Carmarthen Castle, died and the garrison abandoned their stronghold. On hearing the news the Welsh of Brycheiniog, Gwent and Gwynllwg rebelled. In consequence the Normans invaded Gwent, but were defeated at the battle of Celli Darnauc or Kellitravant—an unknown location. Norman forces from Glamorgan then marched into Brycheiniog and devastated the land before founding several unnamed castles. This force then returned whence it had come, but was intercepted and routed at Aberllech, some three miles north-east of Ystrad Glynlais in the mountains between Neath and Sennybridge. Despite this, the Norman strongholds of Pembroke and Breconshire appear to have remained intact.

In the spring of 1097 William Rufus again invaded Wales, this time bringing his forces to bear on the south. No great victory was scored, but the king ordered castles to be built and strengthened, a strategy which appears to have brought about the collapse of the revolt in south Wales. If King William had achieved a victory in south Wales, further defeats in the north meant that Gwynedd and part of Powys were left to the Welsh. War weariness set in and the country was left divided pretty much as it would remain until the fall of Llywelyn ap Gruffydd in December 1282. Welsh kingdoms survived in Gwynedd and Powys and some form of semi-independent existence continued in much of Deheubarth although the Norman hold was now strong in eastern Dyfed, Llandovery, Maelienydd and Breconshire. Glamorgan and Gwent were again firmly under Norman control.

In this atmosphere both the Welsh Kings and Norman Marchers became semi-detached outliers of the kingdom of England, subservient to but independent of the judicial government of the realm. The Marchers held right of life and death, the profits of justice, and the right to form an army from their estates — theoretically for the defence of the country, but often for their own private purposes. As England became once again a country of great wealth and peace under the powerful protection of the Norman kings, the Welsh, Scottish and Norman Marches increasingly became the only areas to have trained and competent soldiers ready for action at short notice.

Ordered Norman Rule, 1100 to 1135

During the reign of William Rufus it is to be assumed that Bernard Neufmarché, William and Philip Braose and their followers strengthened the castles that had been built in Brecknock during the previous three decades. During the period between 1100 and 1103 many grants were made to Brecon Priory, and included those by Picard of Tretower, Richard Le Mans of Humber, and a knight simply called Harold. Walter Cropus granted the tithes of his land of Llansantffraed juxta Usk in Ystrad Yw Uchaf and the church of Cleobury North in Shropshire. Ulger gave his tithes in Wales, while Walter Lyonshall, Roger Baskerville, William fitz Gerald and Robert Devereux granted burgage plots in Brecon. Richard fitz Ralph granted his unidentified land of Firmini and the land of Ralph Cornut. The names of Baskerville, Devereux and Picard turn up again and again in the history of Brecon lordship, whilst all these names probably indicate the owners of castles already built in the honour.

In about 1103, Bernard made a second charter confirming the grants he had made within Honddu (later known as Brecon) Castle. Further gifts were also made by his men, Picard giving his church (probably at Llanfihangel Cwmdu as Tretower seems to have had no church at this time) and land in his homeland (Ystrad Yw Uchaf). Hugh le Wafre also gave the tithes of his unidentified land of Hantune. Both these men and their descendants were to prove instrumental in the history of first Brecon and then Blaenllyfni lordships.

Another early baronial family in Brecknock were the Burghills. In the period 1150 to 1187 William (1165-90+) the son of Robert Burghill, with the consent of his wife Edith, gave to the Priory of St John of Brecon, five acres of land at Fenni near to the road from Brecon to Aberyscir by the river called Gludy.

Another baronial holding in the district of Aberyscir was that held by the Waldeboef family. Between 1191 and 1208 William Waldeboef granted his wood that had previously been held by Bernard Onspac to Brecon Priory. This land, unlike the lordship of Fenni held by the Burghills, lay above the road from Brecon to Aberyscir.

Other honorial divisions of Brecon lordship are equally difficult to disentangle. William Revel was sub-infeudated with (part of?) Hay-on-Wye as a lordship under Bernard Neufmarché in the same manner as the Picards held Tretower and the Baskervilles the mesne lordship of Pencelli. This can be deduced from the third charter of Bishop Bernard of Saint Davids (1115-47), drawn up in the period 1115-21, under which the bishop dedicated the church of St Mary at Hay-on-Wye, and stated that William Revel had endowed that building, with the consent and in the presence of Bernard Neufmarché. This seems to suggest that Neufmarché, or a predecessor, had granted Hay-on-Wye as a fee to William Revel. Despite this, the castle and church evidence suggests that William's fee of Hay did not include his lord's demesne castle of Hay-on-Wye which now so dominates the town. This would explain the closeness of Revel's motte and his church of St Mary, and their distance from the current, and no doubt original, hill-top town and castle of Neufmarché. This might well be the reason for the two castle sites being in close proximity to one another, rather than the site migration theory which is the usually put forward. William Revel does not appear to have had any male heirs and his church of Hay reverted to his overlord on his death, whilst other parts of his lands, later known as Melinog, seem to have passed to a female heir.

In 1121 a scandal arose in Brecon lordship. Mahel, the second son and heir of Bernard Neufmarché, mutilated the paramour of his mother. In vengeance she is said to have sworn that he was the product of an adulterous liaison and by so doing ensured that his sister inherited the family lands. As a consequence, Henry I, who was never adverse to making a crisis work to his advantage, arranged for the marriage of Bernard's daughter, Sibyl, to his friend and confident, Miles Gloucester. He then caused a royal charter to be drawn up between 10 April and 29 May 1121 which empowered Miles Gloucester and Sibyl to hold all the possessions of her father

*Looking across the Wye to Hay, with Hay-on-Wye Castle
in the centre of the picture*

and mother after the death of Bernard Neufmarché and his wife—
or before if they so wished it. The lands of Bernard were then
named: Talgarth, the forest of Ystrad Yw, Hay Castle and all the
land of Brecon up to the land of Richard fitz Pons called Cantref
Bychan, Cowarne in England, and the fees and services of
Bernard's barons, Roger Baskerville [Pencelli], William Revel
[Hay], Robert Turbeville [Maescelyn/Crickhowell] and Picard
[Tretower]. By this charter, and the widely believed perjury of
Agnes Neufmarché, Henry I obtained virtual control of this important barony through the agency of Miles Gloucester. Miles, after the
death of Bernard, enjoyed the barony of Brecon until his own death
in December 1143, although for much of this period he was
engaged in the king's council and, after Henry's death, in wars
against King Stephen (1135-54). Other Neufmarchés seem to have
survived the downfall of the lords of Brecon and to have subsisted
on lands granted to them through marriage by the lords of Gwent,
but in Brecon the future of the barony now lay in other hands.

In the north of Breconshire, the cantref of Buellt was in the
hands of Philip and, after about 1138, another William Braose.
Philip Braose had been temporarily deprived of his English estates
in 1110 at the same time as Count Helias of Maine, who had plotted
against King Henry, was put to death. As the Norman vill of Braose

was on the Maine border, it can be presumed that Philip had aided Helias. Philip was subsequently restored to his lands, probably in February 1113. He died around 1138, having returned from a journey to the Holy Land for which he had departed from Radnor in about 1130. Giraldus tells us that Philip, whom he does not actually name but who he identifies as castellan of Radnor, spent the night in the church of Saint Afan at Llanafan with his hunting dogs. As a result of this sacrilege he went blind, and his dogs mad. As penance for this misdeed he decided to go to Jerusalem, where he was killed in the service of God. However, it is known that Philip Braose survived this journey and the few references to him as lord of Radnor contain no indication that he was blind either before or after his return to the kingdom in around 1133. The story may go towards explaining why his grandson, a yet further William Braose (1175-1211), was said to have been a man of great religion who would not pass a church or wayside cross without dismounting his horse and praying there, much to the annoyance of anyone with whom he was travelling! He was also wont to stop little children in the street merely to hear them answering his greetings with the conventional words of blessing. Such tales hardly bear comparison with other stories of this future 'butcher of Abergavenny'.

Other evidence suggests that the lordship of Buellt was organised on a very different basis to comparable Norman baronies. Radnor, the inherited Braose barony, had been initiated in a standard Norman fashion with knightly tenants owing service at New Radnor Castle. These 'honorial barons' then built castles in their fees. However, in the lordship of Buellt, Philip Braose seems not to have sub-infeudated the land to Norman followers. Instead he apparently ruled the land through Welsh intermediaries, probably of the princely stock of Cadwgan ab Elystan Glodrydd who have continued to hold influence in the land to the present day. The four 'castles' outside of Builth Wells—Caerau, Forest Twdin, Llysdinam and Llanafan—are of such minor construction that they appear either very late in conception, or are the fortifications of Braose lordly tenants of Welsh rather than Norman extraction.

In Brycheiniog during the reign of Henry I, Giraldus tells of a meeting between Gruffydd, the son of King Rhys ap Tewdwr, and Miles Gloucester, the lord of Brecon. As they and Payn fitz John rode past Llangorse Lake it was said that the birds of the lake would not answer their whistles in recognition of the dominion of Miles, but that they instantly followed the call of their true lord, Gruffydd, who now only held the commote of Caeo in Carmarthenshire.

The Anarchy and Earl Miles, 1136 to 1143

The death of King Henry I duly ushered in a power vacuum. According to the Worcester Chronicler, 'in every part of Normandy and England the bond of peace was broken asunder and the greatest disorder prevailed. Every man raised his hand against his neighbour; discord arose, and found its way into the residence of the nobles and wasted the possessions of noble and ignoble. Every man spoiled another of his property: the strong oppressed the weak by force, preventing any complaint being made by threatening further violence; any man resisting being slain. The nobles of a wealthy land, rolling in riches, care little how unjustly the wretched poor are treated; they care only for themselves and their friends. They store their castles and towns with provisions, guard them with an armed military force; their chief fear is some political change. Instead however of having everything settled peaceably out of fear of the king, in many places, especially Wales, depopulations and depredations never cease, and from this one might easily see that England was ruled by governors possessed of small prudence and feeble determination, nay rather by injustice than justice.'

In Brycheiniog, Hywel ap Maredudd seized the opportunity to rebel. Unfortunately there is no certain evidence as to his provenance other than the bald statement that he came from Brycheiniog. He may have belonged to the family of Elystan Glodrydd. On 1 January 1136 Hywel surrounded an Anglo-Norman force from Gower in a loop of the River Lougher and killed 516 knights and footmen in a bloody slaughter, possibly upon Mynydd Carn Goch. He then advanced into the Anglo-Norman lands, destroying churches, towns, wheat and cattle as well as 'burning castles and other fortified places.' In Brycheiniog he was so thorough that the River Wye at Glasbury was said to have run red with the blood of the dead and even 30 years later Giraldus Cambrensis spoke in awe of the damage Hywel had done in the lordship. Whilst this tragedy was unfolding, Miles

Gloucester was at Reading where he was confirmed by King Stephen, Henry I's nephew, as lord of Brecon. In April, Miles was still attending his king while the Welsh must have been putting pressure upon his castle garrisons in central Wales.

With the devastation of Breconshire in progress, Richard fitz Gilbert appeared at Abergavenny on 15 May 1136 on route via Brecon to his lordship of Cardigan. In the town Brian fitz Count warned him of the seriousness of the unrest and offered him an armed escort as far as Brecon. Richard accepted Brian's offer, but on reaching the borders of Gwent and Brecknock and finding nothing amiss he dismissed Brian and his armoured knights, continuing on his journey with his few unarmed followers. It seems from Giraldus' comments that they passed up the valley of the Usk to Tretower Castle and then up the high hill pass towards Castell Dinas. They had not gone far into the woods of Coed Grwyne, apparently with a fiddler and a minstrel leading the party to a jolly tune, when they were intercepted by the troops of Morgan and Iorwerth ab Owain of Caerleon. Lord Richard and his company were soon cut down and the first notable casualty of the Anarchy was obtained within the borders of Brecknock. Many more were soon to follow.

In the aftermath of the battle of Cardigan on 10 October 1136 King Stephen told Miles Gloucester to strike out from Brecon and rescue Richard fitz Gilbert's widow from Cardigan Castle. This Miles duly did, though it is uncertain whether he met any opposition on his chivalric task. A little while later Baldwin fitz Gilbert, Richard's brother, was sent to regain his family lands with a force of lightly armed knights, 500 archers and a purse of royal money. He advanced to Miles' castle of Brecon and there heard that the roads westwards were blocked with felled trees defended by many well prepared men. Baldwin awaited more favourable times, but eventually his money was expended and he retreated in ignominy.

On 10 July 1137 a greater blow befell the Norman defenders of Brecon when Miles' old friend and confidant, Payn fitz John, was hit in the head by a lance and killed whilst he was engaging a Welsh raiding party. Payn's death upset the careful plans of himself and Miles Gloucester in respect to their dominance of south Wales and the border. According to the author of *Gesta Stephani* 'Payn fitz

John and Miles Gloucester during the reign of Henry I, had raised their power to such a pitch that from the River Severn to the sea all along the border between England and Wales they involved everyone in litigation and oppressed them with forced services.' Payn had no male heir so, before his death, he had agreed to the marriage of his daughter and heiress, Cecily, to Roger, the eldest son and heir of Miles Gloucester. To them was to pass the acquisitions of Payn's years of service to the Crown. But Payn's death before the marriage took place left King Stephen with a dilemma. Should he allow the marriage to take place and increase the power of such an already overpowerful baron as Miles Gloucester, or should he insist that some or all of the Lacy lands revert to Gilbert Lacy, the son and heir of the Roger Lacy exiled for treason in 1096. Stephen chose to allow the marriage to go ahead in the winter of 1137, an event that was taken by Gilbert Lacy and his relations as a declaration of war.

At Michaelmas 1139 Earl Robert of Gloucester contacted Miles and his neighbour, Brian fitz Count of Abergavenny, to inform them that the Empress Matilda had arrived in England and hoped for their support in her attempt to take the throne. Miles and Brian signalled their willingness to accept her in the place of her cousin, King Stephen. Miles escorted Matilda from Bristol to his power base at Gloucester and on about 15 October pledged his support.

The opening of hostilities in the Marches saw Miles Gloucester and Geoffrey Talbot besieging Hereford Castle, which they took in February 1140; it is to be presumed that Miles used troops from Breconshire in this campaign. Early in 1141 King Stephen went to Lincoln to try to recover that castle from the earl of Chester who, leaving his brother, William Roumare, to defend the castle, slipped away to the south to join Earl Robert of Gloucester and Miles Gloucester. Together they formed a large army of which one third were Welshmen, and marched against the king at Lincoln. The battle itself resulted in the slaughter of the king's force and the capture of Stephen, but the lightly armed Welsh also suffered heavy casualties.

In Wales the battle seems to have had little effect. Hywel ap Maredudd of Brycheiniog had obviously met his end sometime in the previous four years, and in 1140 his son Maredudd had been slain.

The following year Maredudd's surviving brother, Rhys ap Hywel, was recorded as killing Hywel ap Maredudd ap Rhydderch, the steward of Richard fitz Pons at Llandovery. The same year a grant and confirmation is recorded by Earl Robert of Gloucester which is addressed to Bishop Uthred of Llandaff, Sheriff Robert Norreys of Glamorgan and all his barons and friends, together with the French, English and Welsh of Earl Robert's lands. This document suggests that Welshmen were supporting Earl Robert in his campaigns against King Stephen, and supports suggestions that Miles Gloucester also made agreements with the Welsh. By this means, although the Marcher barons would have lost direct control over much of the hinterlands of their Welsh baronies, they would have achieved a great increase in military strength, adding to their own followings the military might which reinstated Welsh princes could bring into the field. It seems that this arrangement meant Welsh attacks ceased on their and their allies possessions from Cemais through Gower to Glamorgan and Brycheiniog. Indeed in these places, according to a hostile chronicler, Earl Robert kept 'a semblance of peace'.

In England the wheel of fortune meanwhile turned full circle. After King Stephen's capture the Empress Matilda had advanced on London, but met a terrible defeat and was forced to flee west. On 25 July she made Miles Gloucester Earl of Hereford, and he received from Brian fitz Count the lordship of Abergavenny, a powerful addition to his strength in Brecon. On 1 August Matilda's army under Earl Robert of Gloucester began a siege of Winchester which lasted until 15 September, when the Empress was forced once more to retreat. In the rout that followed, Earl Robert was captured and Earl Miles of Hereford only just managed to escape. On 1 November, Earl Robert was exchanged for King Stephen and the kingdom reverted to the state it had been in before the apparently decisive battle of Lincoln.

Matilda's cause suffered another blow when, on 25 December 1143, Earl Miles met his end, transfixed by the arrow of a friend whilst on a hunting expedition in the Forest of Dean. On Earl Miles' death, King Stephen's supporter, Hugh Mortimer of Wigmore, moved against Matilda's supporters in central Wales. The response of Miles' son, Roger, seems to have been rapid and he placed Walter Clifford, the son of the dispossessed Richard fitz

Pons of Llandovery, in charge of Glasbury Castle which was in Roger Tosny's cantref of Elfael. Probably simultaneously, Walter founded Bronllys Castle, which for the next 500 years was to be the administrative centre of Cantref Selyf. At a stroke Walter Clifford had been handed charge of a stretch of land that ran between Earl Roger's Angevin land of Brecon, and Mortimer and Braose's royalist lands of Buellt, Maelienydd and Elfael. The Clifford power in this district was further buttressed by the powerful stone castle at Clifford which Walter held as the steward of Roger Tosny.

The block of land thus placed in the hands of the Cliffords in north Breconshire would seem to have stopped any southward advance of the royalists, but Hugh Mortimer appears to have made an attempt to join forces with Earl Gilbert Clare in Dyfed. If Earl Gilbert and Hugh Mortimer could join hands then Earl Roger of Hereford and Earl Robert of Gloucester would have found them-selves encircled by their enemies and thus isolated might have been crushed. The natural place for the two royalist forces to have met would have been at Llandovery in Cantref Bychan, easily reached from William Braose's land of Buellt and Earl Gilbert's new castle at Dinefwr. It therefore comes as no surprise to find that in 1145 Hugh Mortimer came to blows with Rhys ap Hywel of Brycheiniog and captured him 'after some of his men had been slain and others captured.' The first ally of Earl Roger in Brecknock had been over-whelmed. The junction between the two royalist forces, however, was not to be, for in 1146 Hugh Mortimer seems to have been distracted by trouble in Maelienydd and was eventually defeated.

Revolt and after 1155 to 1165

On the death of King Stephen the crown passed to Matilda's son, Henry Plantagenet of Anjou. He was duly crowned King Henry II on 19 December 1154, almost 19 years to the day after his disas-trous predecessor. One of his first acts as king was to quarrel with Earl Roger over ownership of the tower of Gloucester and other royal demesnes. In the ensuing arguments Earl Roger lost the lord-ship of the castles of Gloucester and St Briavels, but kept both Brecon and Abergavenny intact.

To Earl Roger's north, Hugh Mortimer single-handedly carried on the struggle, munitioning his castles of Wigmore, Cleobury and

Bridgnorth against Henry II. By April King Henry arrived with a royal army swelled by the Welsh troops of Earl Roger's Brecon lordship. Cleobury was taken and after a ferocious three month siege of Bridgnorth Castle, Hugh Mortimer finally came before the royal council and made his peace with the king. This was Roger's last campaign as earl of Hereford, for soon afterwards he went into St Peter's monastery at Gloucester, dying there sometime before 29 September, perhaps as a result of a wound sustained before Bridgnorth. With him died the second short-lived earldom of Hereford, whilst his possessions passed to his brother and heir, Walter Hereford, the Constable.

In 1159 fighting broke out in south Wales as Prince Rhys ap Gruffydd of Deheubarth tried to regain his ancestral lands. The previous year had seen Walter Clifford's castle of Llandovery destroyed and witnessed a massive force chasing Rhys from his siege of Carmarthen Castle. It was possibly in this campaign, or in the successful attempt to rebuild Llandovery Castle by William Beauchamp, that Lord Walter Hereford of Brecon met his end; an entry in the Pipe Roll suggests his death in 1159. He was succeeded by his brother, Henry Hereford.

Effigy of Prince Rhys of Deheubarth

28

A truce made in 1159 seems to have held until 1162 when Prince Rhys again took Llandovery Castle. After this, Bronllys Castle became the Cliffords' westernmost fortress. As a consequence of the breaking of the truce, in early 1163, Henry II invaded south Wales, marching into Dyfed through Glamorgan and returning through Ceredigion, Rhayadr and Radnor, reaching Woodstock by 1 July. It would seem likely that Brycheiniog saw fighting this year when Walter Clifford tried once more to reassert his family interests in Cantref Bychan for he is recorded as having killed Cadwgan ap Maredudd who was probably the son of Maredudd ap Hywel ap Maredudd of Brycheiniog, himself killed in 1140. Fighting in south and west Wales continued through 1164 and into 1165 when, at Easter, Lord Henry Hereford of Brecon met his end, cut down by Prince Seisyll ap Dyfnwal near Castell Arnald, three miles east of Abergavenny. Giraldus says that 'he died a sudden death after a deed of treachery against the Welsh of Abergavenny.' Henry, like his brother before him, had only held the barony of Brecon for some five years.

Henry Hereford was succeeded by his brother Mahel who only held the lordship of Brecon for six months, meeting his end at Bronllys Castle where he had gone to visit his major honourial baron. During the night a fire broke out and as he left the keep a stone fell from its battlements, striking him on the head. The blow proved fatal to the line, for Mahel's only other known brother, William, must have pre-deceased him. So ended the descendants of Earl Miles of Hereford. Both Earl Roger and Henry Hereford had been married, but there had been no offspring of the unions. Neither do any of the brothers seem to have had sons, for all had their charters witnessed by their brothers as heirs.

The lordship of Brecon now passed through the female line to the Braose family of Radnor and Buellt.

The Braose Lords, 1166 to 1206
William Braose inherited the bulk of Earl Miles of Hereford's Welsh estates, receiving Brecon and possibly a little later Abergavenny and some appurtenances in England.

In 1168 war came in force to Breconshire. Rhys ap Gruffydd built a castle at the unidentified Abereynaun, before proceeding on to

Brycheiniog and burning a great part of the land. During this onslaught the castle of Buellt was destroyed, before Rhys made peace with the justiciar of England who had come to stop the offensive.

In 1173 to 74 further rebellions occurred in England, with William Braose, probably both father and son, supporting the king. Prince Rhys had also supported the king, even sending 1,000 troops to Normandy. Indeed, in 1171 King Henry had met Rhys in Dyfed and made him justiciar of south Wales, the start of a personal alliance between the two men that held until Henry's death 18 years later, despite tensions in the period 1182 to 1184. On 29 June 1175 the royal court met at Gloucester where a council was held between the king's men of Wales, both French and English, represented by William Braose, and the Welsh princes, led by Rhys. No leaders of the Welsh are recorded as coming from Brycheiniog but nevertheless, after the peace that was made at Gloucester, Seisyll ap Dynfwal of Gwent and his son Gruffydd (or Geoffrey), together with the heads of many local families, were invited to Abergavenny Castle to hear a royal proclamation. On his guests complaining of the contents of the proclamation, William Braose (thought by most to be the father), had them massacred. He then set out to Castell Arnald and there ripped Cadwaladr, the young son of Seisyll, from his mother's arms and killed him. It was widely believed that Seisyll had been responsible for the death of Henry Hereford, and possibly also of his brother Walter, and that this was Braose's way of gaining revenge. The Welsh principality of Gwent never recovered from this catastrophe, whilst Henry II did nothing about this abuse of his royal peace. Giraldus thought him a conspirator in the affair, as too was reckoned Ralph Poer, the sheriff of Hereford.

In 1182 William Braose (1175-1211) and his army were brought to battle at Dingestow where he was founding a castle—his forces were scattered and he was captured. As he waited to be beheaded a sudden rally by his men caused his captors to look to their own defences and William managed to escape by scrambling down a ditch. Ralph Poer was not so lucky, being killed in the engagement. With this sanguine defeat the Braoses had to accept the reality of the Welsh resurgence in Wales, though their lordship of Brecon still remained a stronghold, increasingly surrounded by hostile Welsh territories. Henry II and his justiciar intervened in the ongoing

Welsh war on several occasions, but the agreement with Rhys ap Gruffydd did not suffer, even when Rhys stated his inability to return to the Marchers the castles his men had taken from them in 1182-84. By 1186 a peace had been restored that even allowed Henry II to ask for Welsh foot serjeants for his wars in France.

In the early March of 1188, the Archbishop of Canterbury, accompanied by Giraldus Cambrensis and Archdeacon Alexander of Bangor, who alone of the clerics could preach in Welsh, toured Wales in search of crusaders to rescue the recently lost city of Jerusalem. To this end they entered Wales on March 4 at New Radnor which had been captured from William Braose in 1182. From here the party went to Crug Eryr Castle in Maelienydd. They left on 7 March and crossed the Wye to Brycheiniog and reached Hay-on-Wye on the same day. Here Giraldus gave a sermon in front of the castle in which the archbishop was staying and where he too probably spent the night. Unfortunately Giraldus says little about the castle except for his implication that it was an ancient fortress. From Hay the preachers went on to Llanddew where they preached and stayed the night, probably in the bishop's castle, the house of Giraldus' own archdeaconry. On 9 March they reached Brecon or Aberhotheni, as Giraldus called it, the place where the Honddu flowed into the River Usk.

At this point in his story Giraldus wrote many stories about William Braose and Matilda St Valery and the knights and inhabitants of Brycheiniog. One of the most interesting in identifying the motte castles which surround Brecon is about a knight called Gilbert Hagurnell. Within Giraldus' own lifetime (1146-1223) this poor knight was said to have suffered from 'a long and unremitting anguish, which lasted three years, and the most severe pains as of a woman in labour, at length gave birth to a calf, an event which was witnessed by a great crowd of onlookers.' Without commenting on the story, or Giraldus' own comments that this was the result of some unnatural vice, the interesting point is that there was a knight near Brecon called Gilbert. It would seem likely that his castle was at Modrydd and is now called Cilwhybert motte. This is almost certainly a corruption of Cil Gilbert and indeed the nearby farmstead is still known as Cwrt Gilbert. The other contender to be lord of this motte was Gilbert Le Mans who has an older provenance. It

Map of Wales showing the main lordships and territories

would also seem likely that if a crowd of people were telling such libellous stories about Gilbert he was not very popular! The Crusade recruitment tour round Wales ended at Chester on 14 April, although most of the trip was spent touring the south.

Of Matilda St Valery, Giraldus records that she had the same powerful religious impulses as her husband as well as being a prudent and chaste woman. He also described her as 'well equipped to rule her household' and 'highly skilled in preserving her property within doors as in increasing it out of doors.'

The death of Henry II on 6 July 1189 ended the period of relative peace. Soon afterwards Rhys launched sustained attacks into Dyfed and besieged Carmarthen. Brecknock seems to have escaped from these early escapades, quite likely due to the personal peace which Rhys had made with William Braose (d.1211), his father having died sometime between 1181 and 1187. This had resulted, towards the end of Henry II's reign, in William's sister, Matilda, marrying Rhys' son and heir Gruffydd. This relationship came to the fore in 1189 when Gruffydd sent his captured brother Maelgwn to be incarcerated by his father-in-law at Brecon. Here Maelgwn remained until 1192 when his father gained his release 'from the prison of the lord of Brycheiniog.'

In the meantime a long running dispute between the lords of Brecon and another co-heir of the Hereford estates had begun, even if it was not to affect Brecknock for another 17 years. Before 1190 Herbert fitz Herbert had married Lucy Hereford, the sister of Bertha and Margaret Hereford. Bertha seems to have been married to Philip Braose of Radnor while Margaret was married to Humphrey Bohun. Theoretically the lands should have been split equally between the three sisters, but in practice this did not occur. The Braoses picked up the lion's share, although the Bohuns received a substantial portion of the English estates. Lucy seems to have obtained nothing but her husband, Herbert, a descendant of Helgot of Holdgate Castle in Shropshire. With the dawning of the reign of Richard I, Herbert made another attempt to obtain their due inheritance and by his death in late 1203 or early 1204 had succeeded in claiming a third of the lands of Margaret Bohun. It was left to Herbert and Lucy's son and heir, Peter fitz Herbert (1204-35), to obtain his third of Brecknock and Gwent Uwch Coed.

During 1190 William Braose (d.1211) did as his father had done, and passed the lordship of Brecon to his son and heir, William Braose (d.1210), upon whom the task of waging war in Wales now fell. In September 1191 William Braose Junior marched eastwards with his Welsh levies and joined Prince John Lackland at Loddon Bridge near Windsor. Here all the nobles of England who had a grudge against the government of Chancellor William Longchamp who ruled in the absence of Richard I on Crusade, assembled and marched on London. Only William Braose is said to have argued in favour of the Chancellor, and this may be the reason for the subsequent hatred Prince and later King John was said to have held for him. By 29 October the Chancellor was forced to flee the country. A new government was set up and a council of nobles and bishops ruled the kingdom until King Richard's return in April 1194.

When the king did return, a William Braose was one of those who met him and accompanied him to Winchester for his second coronation. Richard's return prompted a major campaign in Wales the next year. To the north of Brecknock, Roger Mortimer invaded Radnorshire, William Braose stormed the Dyfed castle of St Clears and Matilda St Valery invaded the principality of Elfael. This was the start of another major war that settled the fate of South Wales for a generation.

The year 1196 saw Rhys ap Gruffydd fighting both William Braoses in Ceredigion, before he set off east, destroying the castles of Colwyn and New Radnor and defeating Roger Mortimer and Hugh Say of Richard's Castle in a set piece battle outside the town. Rhys then moved onto Painscastle where, after besieging the garrison, he came to terms with the Braoses. Breconshire appears to have remained remote from these battles, though it is to be presumed that the Braoses used their Breconshire resources for the campaigns in both east and west Wales.

In April 1197 Prince Rhys died, and was succeeded by his son Gruffyd. Gruffyd was soon captured by Gwenwynwyn of Powys who sold him to the English government. If the English thought they could breathe a sigh of relief, it proved short-lived. For in the north a new prince was rising to power, Llywelyn ab Iorwerth, later to be known as Llywelyn Fawr.

But the Braoses still had trouble holding together their vast domain. In 1198 Painscastle was besieged by Gwenwynwyn and his allies and 'the French' were expelled from Dinefwr Castle by the youngest sons of the Lord Rhys. No doubt these French were the supporters of Matilda Braose, the wife of the imprisoned Gruffydd ap Rhys. In answer to this Gruffydd was released from Corfe Castle in Dorset and joined the English army that assembled at Hay-on-Wye to oppose Gwenwynwyn. This army destroyed the armies of Powys, Gwynedd and Rhwng Gwy a Hafren that were besieging Painscastle—but Gruffydd still had his principality to win back from his brothers. The real beneficiary of the overwhelming victory was the Braose clan, whose power in southern Wales was increased dramatically.

At the opening of the 13th century, strong Braose castles existed at Brecon and Hay-on-Wye, whilst their vassals held their own fortresses at Tretower, Pencelli, Crickhowell, Bwlch y Dinas, Bronllys, Aberyscir and possibly Trecastle. To the north lay the semi-independent Welsh cantref of Buellt, beyond which lay the lands of Elfael and Maelienydd held by the Braoses and the Mortimers respectively. To the south lay another Braose fief at Abergavenny and Monmouth held during the minority of the heir. To the west in Cantref Bychan the old Clifford castle of Llandovery was now in the hands of the feuding descendants of the Lord Rhys. To all intents and purposes the lordship of Brecon seemed secure. The older William Braose (d.1211) was one of the wealthiest barons of England and had estates stretching from Braose in Normandy to St Clears in Dyfed.

At King John's coronation William Senior and his followers were said to have been amongst the king's strongest supporters, support which was greatly rewarded over the next few years. 1199 also saw William's second son, Giles, created bishop of Hereford, further advancing the family.

In 1200, William Senior agreed to pay 700 marks for rights in the barony of Totnes. Other baronies he added to his domain included Gower, with the custody of Glamorgan and the trilateral of Skenfrith, Grosmont and White Castle (which was also claimed and contested by Earl Hubert Burgh of Kent) in 1201, for which he agreed the enormous sum of 800 marks and many beasts. This sum

Crickhowell Castle

was to be paid at £100 per annum, but at the Exchequer the comment was recorded that William 'paid nothing'.

William Senior appeared in the company of King John in Normandy by 28 May 1200, and on 3 June, at Caen, John granted him all the lands he could conquer from the Welsh to augment his barony of Radnor. From this it can be presumed that William was contemplating further campaigns in Elfael and that affairs in Wales were never far from his mind, though William does not seem to have left John's company to continue such conquests.

At Christmas the king and Braose were together near Marlborough, and New Year at Woodstock where Henry I had kept his zoo and Henry II his mistresses. John, too, liked his exotic animals and it is known that he kept lions and leopards here, though these are not quite as exotic as Henry I's porcupine or the elephant Henry III kept at the Tower of London!

Rebellion and War, 1207 to 1218

Despite William Braose Senior's 33 years of sturdy exertion in the cause of his family and the kings of England, 1207 saw the end of his royal service. For some unknown reason, though King John later claimed it was due to William never paying his taxes, the king seems to have demanded several of his castles back from William Braose on the quite valid reason that they were royal castles. This seems to have occurred soon after 24 March 1207, although Glamorgan was in the hands of Faulkes Breauté as early as February. The king's resumption of castles (let alone royal ones) was a royal prerogative which John was entitled to make use of at any time. William Braose seems not to have liked the implication of this demand and began to fortify his castles against the Crown. He then seems to have had second thoughts about what this would entail and subsequently handed over five castles to the king. These fortresses were certainly Carmarthen, Cardigan, Knighton and Norton with the fifth site probably Kington. On 9 April the important castles of Carmarthen and Cardigan were transferred to the custody of William London of Kidwelly, with Knighton and Norton passing into the hands of Robert Sineford, the bailiff of Sheriff Thomas Erdington of Shropshire. With these actions tempers seem to have cooled. During the latter part of 1207 William and his son William Braose Junior were again in the king's company and there seems little indication of the troubles that were soon to rise between them. Indeed on 13 July the king had granted William custody of Ludlow Castle (a Lacy property William had 'bought' the rights to in 1200). William continued to hold it until 19 March 1208 when the king acquiesced in his returning it to his son-in-law, Walter Lacy.

The next stage of the dispute seems to have begun early next year. Firstly the large fines William Braose owed to the king seem to have been at least partially called in. On 29 April 1208, William was ordered to send within 4 days, 1,000 marks to Gerard Athée for the expenses he had incurred during the king's expedition into Wales. Soon afterwards John claimed 5,000 marks of the arrears owed on William's province of Munster and the city of Limerick. These monetary demands were probably only symptoms of the greater trouble brewing between baron and king. On 26 April 1208, with a Papal Interdict in force against England, Bishop Giles Braose of Hereford fled to the Continent with the Primate of England. Consequently on 23 May the king told Walter Clifford to take custody of Hereford Castle and the castles of the bishop of Hereford (Hereford and Lydbury North). At this point Rhys Gryg burned the castle of Llangadog (Luchewein) a second time, taking part of the town from William Braose Senior's nephews, Rhys Ieuanc and Owain ap Gruffydd. In this time of suspicion William Braose, egged on by his wife, refused the king the hostages he demanded of some of his barons to guarantee their continued loyalty. Such actions were treasonable and William acted immediately, probably marching from Brecknock and attacking the castles of Knighton, Norton and Kington that he had surrendered to the king the previous year. The royal garrisons, under Gerard Athée, were obviously aware to the danger and William was frustrated in his purpose.

The king quickly reacted to the threat and appeared in the Marches with an army, causing William Braose Senior to flee with his wife and sons to Ireland where they were harboured by Walter and Hugh Lacy. That William fled so precipitately shows clearly that he did not have the support of his barons in the revolt—without them and their castles William's position immediately became untenable.

With the Braose clan in exile Sheriff Gerard Athée, as *de facto* lord of Brecon, felt free to act against William Braose's Welsh nephews, Rhys Ieuanc and Owain ap Gruffydd. Probably in the autumn he invaded their lands in Buellt. It would seem likely that Gerard formed his army in the valley of the Wye, probably at Bronllys or Hay-on-Wye. From here 'with arrogance and equipped with an excessive amount of arms', he entered the land of Buellt with the intention of laying it waste and fortifying it with castles. His first night was spent at the grange of Aberduhonw at the top of the Wye valley where the lordships of Brecon, Builth, Radnor and Gwrtheyrnion join. The following day he reached the place where he wished to build one of the castles, the site of the new castle at Builth Wells, where the earthworks stand today. Here the sheriff and his Breconshire levies were attacked by the forces of Rhys and Owain together with Iorwerth Clud ab Einion of Elfael. The Welsh chronicle speaks of the sheriff's army having practically separate French and English components—possibly Norman cavalry and English infantry. The battle did not go well for the sheriff and soon the French units were forced to retire back to Aberduhonw Grange. After the whole day had been spent in conflict, the English were finally forced to surrender. So ended the first attempt to re-conquer Buellt.

On the aftermath of this defeat, Prince Gwenwynwyn of Powys attacked Peter fitz Herbert who, with the flight of the Braose clan, had finally been granted a third of Brecknock by King John. As a result of Gwenwynwyn's attack, on 29 September the king ordered 'all his bachelors and lieges to his aid.' Gwenwynwyn at this point seems to have had second thoughts about pushing home his attack and went to plead his case before King John. John, not taking kindly to this attack on a man whom he had just honoured with a third of an important barony, imprisoned the luckless prince of Powys at Shrewsbury. In the meantime Prince Llywelyn ab Iorwerth moved against Gwenwynwyn's now leaderless forces and threw his ally Prince Maelgwn ap Rhys of Deheubarth out of Ceredigion. Llywelyn then transferred this province to William Braose's nephews, Rhys Ieuanc and Owain ap Gruffydd.

The next year Rhys and Owain, maintaining their advantage, moved against their uncle Rhys Gryg and evicted him from Llangadog Castle once more. King John by this time had determined to settle the Braose and Welsh problem once and for all. On 20 July 1209 he marched westwards with a large feudal host, forced Rhys and Owain to submit and exiled them to Ireland. By the end of July the king was free to mount a brief and successful campaign in Scotland, in which he was accompanied by Llywelyn ab Iorwerth.

The unity suddenly displayed in Wales proved, as ever, illusory. King John consequently decided to take the war to the Braoses in Ireland. On 17 June 1210 he landed at Waterford and soon forced Walter Lacy to surrender and Matilda St Valery and her sons and daughters to flee to Scotland where they were intercepted in Galloway and captured; William Braose Senior had meantime returned to Wales.

Engelard Cigogné, who had replaced Gerard Athée as sheriff of Gloucester, was now custodian of the Braose lands in Wales and set out to complete what his predecessor had tried to do two years previously. He marched his army, probably consisting largely of men from the lordship of Brecon, up the Wye valley and arrived, like his predecessor, at Builth Wells. Here, as before, a battle was fought and some 40 Englishmen were killed. However, the Welsh casualties must have been much heavier for this time Buellt was conquered and the sheriff constructed castles at Gaer Loyw (possibly Caerau) and Builth Wells.

On 8 September Prince Rhys Gryg, supported by royal troops, forced Llandovery Castle, held by men loyal to Rhys Ieuanc and Owain ap Gruffyd, to surrender. On 20 September William Braose Senior, his allies all defeated or captured, met King John at Bristol and offered him 40,000 marks to regain his lands and the liberty of his family. Matilda St Valery scornfully rejected this plea and William, fearing the worst, fled to his port of Shoreham in Sussex and thence in disguise to France. Matilda and her son, William Braose Junior, were starved to death in Windsor Castle, while, on 9 August 1211, the older William Braose died in Paris, a broken man, though he was accorded the honour of being buried in St Victor's Abbey, a Welsh Marcher abroad. His nephews Rhys and Owain had meanwhile been forced out of central Wales and in the first half of September 1211 they surrendered their last lands around Aberystwyth.

This total overthrow of the house of Braose presented King John with a wealth of land to redistribute, and it is noticeable that he favoured his foreign mercenaries like Faulkes Breauté, Gerard Athée and Walter Teuton, rather than the old baronial families of the March. Brecon itself remained in the hands of the sheriff of Gloucester.

The following year saw the tide turn against King John in Wales. After Prince Llywelyn had spent Easter with the king at Cambridge, he determined once more to rebel. On 26 May 1212 the king ordered the reinstatement of Rhys Ieuanc and Owain ap Gruffydd, their uncle, Maelgwn, having thrown in his lot with Prince Llywelyn's rebellion. The war did not start well for the king and Robert Vipont was rapidly surrounded in his new castle of Mathrafal in Powys. On 26 July Engelard Cigogné was ordered to break the siege and relieve Robert. This he achieved on about 4 August and it is to be presumed that he took the levy of Brecknock with him on this campaign. In the meantime Faulkes Breauté, now sheriff of Glamorgan, was ordered to supply the needs of Rhys Ieuanc and Owain ap Gruffydd in their war against the rebels. Presumably by their loyalty to John they intended to regain their hereditary lands in Deheubarth as well as their mother's inheritance of Buellt, now in the hands of Engelard Cigogné.

Engelard Cigogné and Faulkes Breauté no doubt did their part in helping Rhys Ieuanc to reclaim his lands, as can be adjudged from the battle of Llandeilo which occurred towards the end of January 1213. Rhys Ieuanc had formed an Anglo-Welsh army in Brecknock and marched westwards towards his old stronghold of Llandovery, making camp soon after 21 January at Trallwng Elgan north of Talley in Ystrad Tywi. The next day he was joined by his brother Owain ap Gruffydd, Faulkes Breauté, and probably Engelard Cigogné. The army marched off the following morning in three divisions, the van being led by Rhys, Faulkes being in the centre and Owain bringing up the rear. Just before the town of Llandeilo they were met by the army of Rhys Gryg and a battle ensued. After a stiff fight Rhys Gryg left his men and burned the town of Llandeilo to deny it to the enemy. He then left a garrison in Dinefwr and Llandovery Castles and retired westward towards his brother Maelgwn who was also opposing the king. Rhys Ieuanc, after taking Dinefwr Castle by direct assault, retired to Brycheiniog and raised yet another Franco-Welsh force with which to assault Llandovery Castle. On seeing his arrival, the garrison promptly surrendered 'on condition that they should be granted their lives and their members.' The nephews of William Braose Senior and the knights of Brecknock were having their day and on 29 April 1213 the king ordered Faulkes Breauté to hand the land which used to belong to Maelgwn ap Rhys over to Rhys Ieuanc ap Gruffydd and to offer him all the support he could. In their moment of triumph the strife was brought to an end by the truce negotiated by the Papal Legate at the instance of the Pope on 3 June 1213.

The year 1214 passed in an uneasy Welsh truce while King John unsuccessfully tried to regain Normandy from King Philip Augustus of France. Amongst the royal advisors at this time was Bishop Giles Braose, readmitted to royal circles with John's surrender to the Pope in 1213. On 5 March 1215 the king accepted Bishop Giles' fine for his father's English and Welsh lands, but by April civil war had broken out in England and on 10 May John virtually admitted that he was intending to continue in his possession of Brecknock during the disturbances. For Giles this seems to have proved intolerable and on 15 May he rebelled, John at once ordering sequestration of his Gloucestershire estates. In reply the bishop sent his brother Reginald Braose to Brecknock to reclaim the family lands. Within three days Reginald had gained possession of the castles of Pencelli in Brecknock and Abergavenny, White Castle and Skenfrith in Gwent. When Giles himself arrived some little time later all of Brecon Lordship including the castles of Brecon, Hay, Blaenllyfni [held by Peter fitz Herbert as an independent barony] and Builth Wells together with Radnor Castle went over to him.

Meanwhile Rhys Ieuanc and his brother Owain made peace with their uncle, Maelgwn ap Rhys, and on 27 May attacked the royalist barony of Cemais. On 2 July, having agreed to the Magna Carta in June, the king, in an attempt to forestall the still growing Welsh rebellion, invited Bishop Giles Braose to a friendly conference. These peaceable moves did not stop the war and by 6 August Peter fitz Herbert of Blaenllyfni had joined Giles and Reginald Braose in their rebellion. On 9 October a further safe conduct was issued to Bishop Giles Braose who, on 21 October, under papal pressure of suspension, made peace with the Crown during the siege of Rochester Castle. But Giles died on 17 November as he was returning to the Marches, leaving his last surviving brother, Reginald, as *de facto* lord of Brecon. Meanwhile, in a very mild winter, Prince Llywelyn led an army south that included Rhys Ieuanc and Owain ap Gruffydd and overran much of south-west Wales by Christmas. Llewelyn and Reginald cemented their tentative alliance when Reginald married Llewelyn's daughter, Gwladys Ddu.

On 27 July 1216 King John appeared in person at Hay-on-Wye where the princes of Elfael under Gwallter ab Einion Clud came to him to pay homage on 29 July. Afterwards he burned the castle and town and set off northwards through the mountains of Elfael to Radnor. Reginald Braose and most of his barons remained unmoved in their Brecknock fastnesses.

The Last Braose Lords of Brecon, 1217 to 1233

King John died on 19 October 1216 and the kingdom passed to his young son Henry III, with Earl William Marshall, Earl of Pembroke, leading the regency council. Throughout the winter war raged between the royalists and the rebels who had now espoused the cause of Louis, the dauphin of France. By the summer of 1217 the issue had been settled and even the most staunch of the rebels had made their peace. On 23 June Reginald Braose submitted to the

Crown and was confirmed in his lands. As news of Reginald's peace reached Wales, his cousins Rhys Ieuanc and Owain ap Gruffydd 'rose up and won from Reginald the cantref of Buellt and three castles', probably Caerau (possibly the Gaer Loyw of 1210), Llanafan, and either Forest Twdin or Llysdinan. Reginald's cousins were not the only Welsh princes enraged by his defection, for Llywelyn himself advanced into Brycheiniog to punish his errant son-in-law, with the intention of burning Brecon. But he was met by the burgesses, who used the good offices of Rhys Ieuanc to negotiate with the prince and obtained a peace for 100 marks whilst supplying 5 hostages for their future good behaviour.

On 13 July Peter fitz Herbert, the old friend of King John, also returned to the royal cause and on 24 July Earl William ordered Reginald Braose, lord of Brecon, to restore Blaenllyfni Castle, occupied by him in the last war, to Peter. This strongly suggests that there was still rivalry between the two men and that Reginald had been keeping Peter out of Brecknock since the rebellion of 1215, even though they had been fighting for the same rebel cause. A baron of Brecknock who disappears during this period is William Waldeboef, the probable lord of Aberyscir Castle and constable of Brecon. He seems to have been succeeded by his son John, but the constableship of Brecon passed to William Burghill of nearby Fenni, another long time supporter of the lords of Brecknock.

The year 1218 began inauspiciously for Reginald Braose. In January John, Giles, Philip and Walter Braose, the children of William Braose Junior, together with their mother, Matilda Clare, were released from royal custody. John Braose for one was intent on claiming all his grandfather's lands from his uncle Reginald. Indeed, Reginald appears to have been out of royal favour, for he was never named amongst the Marchers instructed to carry out any orders in the king's name. This view is reinforced on 26 January 1219 when the sheriff of Hereford, Hugh Mortimer of Wigmore, Robert Mortimer of Richard's Castle, Walter Clifford Junior, his brother Roger, and John Monmouth were informed that the Three Castles of the justiciar (Skenfrith, Grosmont and White Castle) had been adjudged against Reginald Braose as the property of Hubert Burgh. Further, these barons were to take the castles from Reginald by force if he did not hand them over without delay. Such an instruction does not have the tone of a particularly friendly government.

Matters were made worse for Reginald when on 7 March 1219 John Braose began legal proceedings against his uncle to claim the honours of Brecon, Elfael, Buellt, Radnor, Kingsland, Gwent, Abergavenny, Skenfrith, Grosmont and White Castle. Reginald, after abandoning the castles of the Trilateral to Hubert Burgh, seems not to have relinquished the surrounding lands and shortly after 4 July it was recorded that he was destroying the woods of Skenfrith and Grosmont in opposition to Hubert Burgh. No doubt this chopping down of woods was also to aid in the refortification of his many castles in the Welsh Marches, some of which had been heavily damaged in the past few years. A few days later, on 10 July, Reginald appeared at Shrewsbury with Prince Llywelyn to answer the pleas of John Braose and his mother Matilda in front of the Papal Legate Pantulf. It was probably soon after Llywelyn's meeting with John and Matilda Braose that Rhys [Mechyll ap Rhys] Gryg married 'a daughter of the earl of Clare'. As his wife was also called Matilda Braose, it is easy to see that this woman was the recently released Matilda Braose née Clare. To further cement the new alliance John Braose married Margaret, the daughter of Llywelyn ab Iorwerth. In two fell swoops Llywelyn had firmly attached the enemies of Reginald Braose, his now disagreeable son-in-law, to his own cause. However, the further alienation of Reginald from Llywelyn in turn meant that Reginald became more popular at court as an enemy and possible buffer against Llywelyn. Thus it is no surprise to find, on 2 December, the sheriffs of Gloucester, Worcester and Hereford being told by the Crown to send men to aid Reginald Braose in fortifying 'his castle of Buellt and to make trenches or paths and ditches there against our enemies.'

The years 1220-1222 appear to have been peaceful in Brecknock, but early in September 1223, as part of a wider war, Llywelyn moved against Reginald Braose, and besieged Builth Wells Castle. In England the feudal levy was called out and advanced to Bronllys Castle, the threat proving sufficient to bring Llewelyn to terms.

In the meantime Rhys Gryg and Maelgwn ap Rhys paid homage to Henry, whilst several Marchers including Roger Picard of

Tretower, John Waldeboef of Aberyscir, David Burghill of Fenni and Ystrad Yw, Henry Fraxino of Presteigne, and Robert Burghill, were liberated from Llywelyn's prison. Llywelyn's war in Brycheiniog can be seen from this to have been not entirely unsuccessful—it was merely his inability to hold his own in three theatres of war simultaneously (along the Shropshire borders and in southwest Wales in addition to the Middle March) that forced him to the treaty table.

With this truce, major warfare in Brycheiniog was brought to an end for several years. Reginald Braose became intimately involved in the government of the realm, before his death in early June 1228. On 13 July, William, his son and heir, was granted his castles of Radnor and Huntington. It is presumed that he was already holding Brecknock as his father's heir as this was never mentioned in any contemporary royal documents.

William Braose did not long hold his father's lands. By August 1228 Montgomery Castle was heavily besieged by the local Welsh. A truce was made with Llywelyn on 15 August whereby William Braose was to be one of the barons who accompanied Llywelyn's wife, Princess Joan, to Shrewsbury where she was to carry out negotiations with the king on behalf of her husband. The negotiations seem to have proved abortive for on 25 September the king marched on Ceri where he wrote to all the tenants of Elfael informing them that their lord, William fitz Reginald Braose, had been captured by Llywelyn. The capture of the new lord of Brecon proved merely a prelude to his fall.

William Braose remained incarcerated until 12 February 1229, when the king agreed to the terms of his release. These terms included £2,000 [which just happened to be the same amount Llywelyn owed the king] and the cantref of Buellt with its castle as a dower for his daughter, Isabella, to marry Llywelyn's son and heir, Dafydd. With this agreement struck and ratified between prince, marcher lord and king, on 5 September Fulk fitz Warin and the bishop of Hereford were designated by the king to escort Prince Dafydd and his sister Gwladys Ddu, the widow of Reginald Braose, to Westminster to do homage.

In the meantime a devious plot was hatched between William Braose and Princess Joan, Llewelyn's wife, the illegitimate daughter of King John. The details will probably never be known, but it was thought in Government circles that William Braose, after starting an affair with Joan, plotted to kill Llewelyn. As a consequence, Hubert Burgh, fearing for the safety of the prince, and certainly wishing to damage a powerful neighbour with whom he had many disputes, informed Llywelyn of the plot. Llywelyn acted swiftly and one night when William Braose had come to his court, which he had often been doing ostensibly to arrange the marriage between his daughter Isabella and Llywelyn's son Dafydd, the prince burst into his wife's bed chamber and found the two in a compromising position. William was thrown into irons.

On 20 April, the king ordered that the constables of Radnor, Hay, Huntington, Brecon and Abergavenny should turn over their castles to Peter fitz Herbert of Blaenllyfni and John Monmouth, as William Braose and his knights had been imprisoned by Llywelyn. But after some further thought, on 25 April the king countermanded the order and granted the lands and castles into the custody of William Marshall.

After a short trial before the baronage of Wales on 2 May, William Braose was hung before 800 people at the manor of Crogen (Crokein). Soon afterwards Llywelyn wrote to William Braose's widow Eva, to seek her confirmation for the proposed marriage between their children, Dafydd and Isabella. In the meantime, to enforce his claim to Buellt, Llywelyn marched into the cantref and, according to the *Worcester Chronicle*, thoroughly demolished Builth Wells Castle.

Owain ap Goronwy was appointed Llywelyn's constable of Buellt and he soon found it necessary to order William fitz Adam Christchurch, the king's representative at Brecon, to let Madog Vaughan of Llangynog clear away his crops, cut flax and mow his hay in his lands in Brecknock, probably around Castell Madog, or face the possibility of war. William Christchurch in turn complained to the Chancellor that although Llywelyn held to the truce, his men, especially Madog Vaughan, did not. Madog and his men of Buellt were also holding two Brecknock men prisoner and had 'plundered' three others. Correspondence between Christchurch and the Chancellor continued over the aggravation, during which time, on 8 April 1231, Brecon, Abergavenny,

Huntington and Radnor Castles with the lands of William Braose and the Earl Marshall that were held by William Christchurch were all made over to John Monmouth and Walter Clifford. This was followed on 11 April by the order for John Monmouth and Walter Clifford to hand custody of the lands of William Braose over to Earl Richard of Cornwall. Then on 16 April they were again granted the lands of William Marshall in custody.

Soon after this muddled set of instructions and counter instructions, Llywelyn, and no doubt also his ally Madog Vaughan of Llangynog, began to attack Brecknock, incensed by the beheading of certain prisoners who were probably his envoys returning from England. About 21 May Hubert Hoese, the new royal commander at Brecon, wrote to the king concerning Brecon Castle, the custody of which he understood was to be handed over to Walter Clifford. Subsequently, on 25 May the knights the king had ordered to defend Brecon and Abergavenny Castles were ordered to serve under Walter Clifford.

The war began soon after with Llywelyn burning the town of Montgomery, sacking Radnor and its castle, and marching on Hay-on-Wye which was put to sword and flame. The castle held out, and Llewelyn moved on to Brecon where the town and priory felt his fury. Once more the castle held out, and Llywelyn advanced into Gwent and burnt Caerleon. Neath Castle was taken by the prince around 29 June and this was soon followed by the fall of Kidwelly. It was not without reason that the Tewkesbury annalist wrote that this was the year when Llywelyn conquered all Wales!

The high point of the war for Llywelyn probably came on 22 July when it was reported to Walter Godardville, the custodian of Hay-on-Wye Castle, that Llywelyn was with a small force on the north bank of the River Wye. His informant, a monk of Abbey Cwmhir, also told Walter that there was a little-known ford across the river which would allow him to take Llywelyn by surprise. Such a prize blinded Walter to the reality of the situation, and, accepting the monk's assurances as to the fordability of the river, he set off in hot pursuit of his prey. As Walter's heavy cavalry crossed the river it soon became apparent that all was not what the monk had said. The horses, weighed down by armour and men, floundered in the riverside mud, and the waiting Welsh army fell in ambush upon the stranded horsemen. In the resulting carnage Reginald fitz Richard Argenten, his brother and three other nobles were captured and 300 knights were said to have been killed. When King Henry, rebuilding nearby Painscastle in Radnorshire, heard of the disaster he fined the monks of Cwmhir 300 marks to save their grange of Carnass from being burned down.

The war continued through the autumn and on 5 October 1231 Walter Lacy, Walter Clifford (who was now holding much of Brecknock), Ralph Mortimer of Wigmore, William Stuteville of Richard's Castle, William fitz Warin of Whittington and John fitz Alan of Clun, were ordered to attack the king's enemies, provision their castles for siege and rescue any castles that were attacked. Such orders, without money or men to carry them out, were meaningless and on 27 October Earl Richard of Cornwall was mandated to go to the Marches of Wales to make a truce with Llywelyn.

In Brecknock the removal of William Braose should have left the door open for John Braose to reassert his claim to the Brecon lordship. If he did put forward any claim it was cut short for, a little before 16 July 1232, he fell from his horse at the family home of Bramber Castle and was dragged to his death. His children were never able to press their claim to Brecon as it was several years before they came of age and by then other barons had taken their place in Brecon lordship.

The year 1232 passed in relative peace, but it proved to be a lull before the next storm. In early 1233 Llywelyn broke the truce and attacked the Braose lands which were now in the custody of Earl Richard of Cornwall. Richard is said to have defeated Llywelyn, but after this apparently minor skirmish things began to go increasingly wrong for the Crown. A confederacy of the barons was formed under Earl Richard Marshall and which included Walter Clifford, the mesne lord of Cantref Selyf, to oppose the clique of Poitevins governing the country for Henry III. War broke out between the two factions sometime after 22 May.

By 31 July 1233 severe unrest had been reported in Herefordshire and the king ordered the sheriff to arrest any armed bands, presumably those of Walter Clifford and his followers. Henry III brought the royal army to the Marches, basing himself at Hay-on-Wye at the beginning of September, and the Clifford castles

*Bronllys Castle as depicted in 1805; Castell Dinas lies on
the prominent knoll behind*

soon fell into royal hands. On 1 September the king ordered the
custody of Bronllys Castle to be passed from the royalist Baldwin
Gisnes to Sheriff William fitz Warin of Hereford, and gave the land
and castle of Aberllyfni that had until recently belonged to Hugh
Kinnersley, a knight of Walter Clifford, to one Inges the crossbowman. At this point Hugh himself seized the castle back from its
royal garrison and once more raised the flag of revolt, munitioning
the castle against the king. The constable of Hay was immediately
ordered to take it back. Clifford Castle surrendered on 3 September
and on 17 September Walter Clifford made his peace with the king.

Soon after 14 October 1233, Prince Llywelyn and Owain ap
Gruffydd attacked again. First to feel their anger was the town of
Monmouth which was burned. Then they moved northwards and
cut a swathe through Brycheiniog destroying in turn the castles of
Abergavenny, Tretower, Blaenllyfni, Pencelli and Bwlch y Dinas
before 29 October. The princes then sacked and burnt Brecon town
while they besieged the castle with catapults and siege engines for

49

a month. The princes and Earl Richard Marshall, still in rebellion, deciding that Brecon Castle was not going to fall, then set off for the north and on the way burnt the town of Clun, destroyed Ruthin Rygantin Castle and burnt the town of Oswestry. Meanwhile Llywelyn's Marcher allies took Cardiff Castle on 15 October.

On 11 November Llywelyn's forces surprised Henry III at Grosmont and shattered the royal army, sending many fleeing for their lives in their night attire and leaving their horses and armour to the victorious Welsh. In response, by 10 January garrisons had been installed in the previously sacked Brecknock castles of Blaenllyfni and Bwlch y Dinas and the garrison in Hay-on-Wye had been strengthened. This was despite the claims of the *Welsh Chronicles* that all the castles of Brycheiniog had succumbed — Hay and Brecon at least and no doubt Bronllys had survived the storm. In addition, Walter Teuton, King Henry's favourite German soldier, was ordered to let Walter Clifford have 100 Welsh foot serjeants and 10 horse serjeants to swell the forces he already had at Bronllys to keep the peace in those parts. Walter Clifford's presence at Bronllys in October may well have halted Llywelyn's victorious march to the east and possibly even checked the assault on Brecon. The lord of Clifford was clearly back in full royal favour and now reverted to his original role, that of the major mesne baron of Brecon. Once more it was his job to protect the land from hostile attack from the west.

But by February 1234 the war in Wales was over for the present, and before 14 March 1234 Walter Clifford left the Marches and began witnessing royal charters at Woodstock. Thomas Kinnersley of Aberllyfni made his peace on 13 March, and his brother Hugh was reinstated in his land of Aberllyfni on 5 April 1234 after agreeing to pay a fine of 20 marks, which was duly rendered on 20 May. On 31 May Henry Turbeville was ordered to deliver to Eva Braose, the sister of Richard Marshall and widow of the last William Braose, her castle and land of Hay-on-Wye, previously in royal hands.

To finalize the peace, the Treaty of Myddle was signed between Llywelyn and the king on 7 July 1234. This agreed to a truce for two years and recognized the *status quo* as it existed before the Earl Marshall's conquests.

The arms of Braose and Bohun

Earl Humphrey Bohun of Hereford, 1236 to 1262

Prince Llywelyn died on 10 April 1240. Immediately his heir, Prince Dafydd, to whom the Welsh princes had sworn homage at Strata Florida in October 1238, captured and incarcerated his brother Gruffydd together with his eldest son Owain Goch. Llywelyn ap Gruffydd, however, seems to have been allowed his liberty. Early in May Dafydd and his barons went to Gloucester to do homage to his uncle, Henry III. The meeting resulted in the Treaty of Gloucester by which Dafydd agreed to subject all the still disputed lands in Wales to an arbitration made by the bishops of Worcester, Norwich and St Asaph, Earl Richard of Cornwall, John Monmouth, Ednyfed Fychan and Einion Fychan with the papal legate, Otto, presiding over them. No sooner was this agreement made and Dafydd returned to Wales, than King Henry began distributing the disputed lands seemingly without reference to the proposed arbitration. Thus Brecon was apportioned out to Earl Humphrey Bohun for his son Humphrey and his wife Eleanor Braose, and Maelienydd to Lord Ralph Mortimer of Wigmore. The repeated mentions of Roger Picard in the preceding few years may also suggest that he now held a front line interest in the Anglo-Welsh wars and that the border was much closer to his stronghold at Tretower than it has previously been recognised.

As a result of ill-will over this distribution of lands, war broke out in June 1241. Walter Clifford was one of the barons with the royal army which, on 24 August, forced Dafydd to surrender at Gwern Eigron, two miles south of Rhuddlan. Defeated, Dafydd agreed to restore to the barons of the March their lands lost since the days of King John. He also allowed the homage of the Welsh barons to be rendered to Henry as they had been previously. Further, Ellesmere was given to the king and Dafydd agreed not to receive outlaws from England. The prince of Gwynedd then restored Gruffydd ap Gwenwynwyn to his hereditary lands in Powys and the sons of Maredudd ap Cynan to their lands in Meirionydd. After this surrender it was quite rightly said in several monastic chronicles that the Marchers had regained their lands in Wales. On 3 September Gruffydd ap Llywelyn was escorted from his prison at Criccieth to the Tower of London as surety for Dafydd's good behaviour.

During the summer of 1242, John Monmouth fortified the castle of Builth Wells for the king which, whilst ruined, should have come to Dafydd together with the surrounding cantref as his just marriage portion. With this act of injustice the matter of Brecknock was allowed to rest for the time being, but there could be little doubt that Dafydd would dispute the issue again once he was strong enough. That time came sooner than anyone would have thought.

On 1 March 1244, Gruffydd ap Llywelyn was killed whilst trying to escape from the Tower of London on a rope of knotted bed sheets and soon after Dafydd rose once more. His initial campaign was against Gruffydd ap Madog of Bromfield, Gruffydd ap Gwenwynwyn of Powys and Morgan ap Hywel of Gwynllwg, hoping to gain their submission. The rising was initially opposed by the earl of Clare, Earl Humphrey Bohun of Hereford who was now in all but name lord of Brecon, John Monmouth, and other Marchers. Henry III, after his easy victory in 1241, seemed unconcerned at events in Wales, focussing his attention instead on Scotland. Only slowly did the seriousness of the Welsh revolt begin to sink in. Exactly what happened in Buellt at this time is difficult to judge, but Dafydd seems to have successfully taken the cantref even if the castle did not fall. In a document dated to the war of 1244-5 Dafydd tells his bailiffs of Buellt—Rhys ap Hywel, William Fychan, Llywelyn ap Gruffydd (the future prince of Wales?) and Madog Fychan (of Llangynog?)—that he had once again taken

Dore Abbey, in Herefordshire, under his protection. This would suggest that his troops were pushing south from Llangynog into the Dore granges of Gwenddwr and Llaneglwys.

According to Matthew Paris, who was a contemporary of the events he related, Dafydd attacked Ralph Mortimer and Earl Humphrey Bohun for holding Brecon, Huntington and Hay-on-Wye which Dafydd had claimed by right of his wife, Isabella Braose, and which the Marchers claimed in right of their own Braose heiresses. This would suggest heavy fighting in Radnorshire and Brecknock.

In the meantime, on 26 April 1245 the sheriff of Hereford was ordered to equip and munition Builth Wells Castle together with Painscastle, and between 13 July and 29 August John Monmouth received £60 for this work. On 26 August the earl of Hereford wrote that with the help of William Cantilupe of Abergavenny, Walter Clifford of Cantref Selyf, Ralph Mortimer of Wigmore and William Stuteville of Richard's Castle and their men he had attacked the Welsh forces between Brecon and Shrewsbury. In the meantime, Henry III marched an army to the River Conway. For three months this army lay encamped in its linen tents at Degannwy under constant night attack and short of victuals and warm clothing. On 24 September there was a heavy slaughter of the English in an ambush. Henry III was losing men and gaining little. On 21 October 3,000 foot serjeants arrived from Ireland, but just six days later Henry withdrew. Behind him he left a strengthened Degannwy Castle 'like a thorn in Dafydd's eye'.

On 26 July Pope Innocent IV had supported Dafydd's claim that Henry III had wantonly cast arbitration aside in favour of war in 1241. Consequently the next year Henry had the case quashed after sending an envoy to the pope with his, and Earl Humphrey Bohun's, own version of events. However, sometime before 25 February 1246, Dafydd died at Aber, being succeeded by his nephew, Llywelyn ap Gruffydd. Immediately his elder brother Owain Goch, who had been under royal protection at Shotwick, sought to seek his share of the inheritance. In the meantime, in this period of uncertainty, several Welsh nobles submitted to the king and on 21 April the abbot of Basingwerk was instructed to escort Isabella Braose, Dafydd's widow, from Dyserth Castle, where she was in the custody of Philip le Bret, to 'live honourably' at Godstow Nunnery. The current war was nearing its end.

Once more a period of peace and prosperity came to Brycheiniog, divided though it was—the cantref or lordship of Buellt was held for the Crown by royal appointees; two-thirds of Brecon lordship, which included Brecon, Hay-on-Wye and Huntington castles, together with the honourial Clifford held castle of Bronllys, was held by Earl Humphrey Bohun of Hereford for his son Humphrey Junior and his wife Eleanor Braose; the other third of Brycheiniog was held by Herbert fitz Peter as the lordship of Blaenllyfni. This included his demesne castles of Dinas and Blaenllyfni and the major sub-lordship castles of Pencelli, Maescelyn/Crickhowell and Tretower.

During this quiet period, Reginald succeeded his brother, Herbert fitz Peter at Blaenllyfni and Roger Picard was succeeded at Tretower by his son, another Roger, who in 1252 was granted a respite of knighthood on payment of a fine of 6 gold coins (bezants).

Sometime between October 1249 and March 1250, Gwladys Ddu, the widow of both Reginald Braose and Ralph Mortimer, demanded her dower lands from Earl Humphrey Bohun. In 1250 the young Roger Mortimer of Wigmore and Matilda Braose, his wife, claimed against Walter Cantilupe of Abergavenny and his wife and Humphrey Bohun Junior of Brecon and Eleanor, his wife, a reasonable part of the lands and tenements of William Braose, their wives' father. The Mortimer claim to a third of the remains of Brecon and Abergavenny baronies had begun. Most interestingly no claim was raised against Reginald fitz Peter in Blaenllyfni. From this we can see that this part of Bernard Neufmarché's old barony had been irretrievably divided from Brecon lordship.

On 24 February 1252 the partition of the Braose inheritance was formally undertaken by the abbot of Pershore. First he fulfilled his intention of valuing all the lands which had belonged to the last William Braose and then he partitioned them amongst William's three heiresses, Matilda the wife of Roger Mortimer, Eve the wife of William Cantilupe and Eleanor the wife of Humphrey Bohun Junior. As a result, Humphrey Bohun Junior was confirmed in his land of Brecon, William Cantilupe received Abergavenny and Roger Mortimer Radnor and Presteigne. This split, which Roger

Mortimer felt was less than his fair share, would bring trouble between the three for many years. Adding to his chagrin, on 29 November John Monmouth was ordered to relinquish his constableship of Builth Wells Castle to William Cantilupe, placing another part of the Braose inheritance in hands other than Roger's. It is obvious from a subsequent grant to the young Lord Edward, eldest son of Henry III, of 14 February 1254 that the king now regarded Buellt as a royal escheat and not part of the Braose estates, even though it had been one of their oldest possessions.

This grant to Edward was part of a large Welsh estate which included Rhuddlan, Dyserth and Degannwy with the other lands of the Perfeddwlad, the trilateral of Skenfrith, Grosmont and White Castle, Montgomery, Carmarthen and Cardigan. But Edward's oppressive fiscal policy led, at the end of October 1256, to two Welsh princes, Llywelyn and Dafydd ap Gruffydd, forming an army and invading the Perfeddwlad. A month later, on 6 December 1256, Prince Llywelyn granted Maredudd ab Owain, the son of William Braose Senior's nephew, Edward's portion of Ceredigion and the land of Buellt. They then invaded Buellt which 'they occupied with a strong hand.' To counter this 10 wooden crossbows, 8 crossbow belts, a rope for the well and other equipment were delivered to Richard Thunderley, the constable of Builth Wells Castle.

Walter Clifford, like his contemporaries, began to raise his forces against the old enemy. John Grey of Wilton was appointed by Prince Edward to keep the March of Wales between the county of Chester and south Wales, and subsequently Earl Humphrey Bohun was given custody of the Marches from Montgomery to Gloucester, supported by, amongst others, Roger Mortimer of Wigmore, Walter Clifford, Humphrey Bohun Junior of Brecon and Reginald fitz Peter of Blaenllyfni. Despite this activity a triple royal campaign of 1257 proved ineffective. The heavens opened and during July torrential rains and floods blocked the passage of the armies and those actions that did take place all favoured Llywelyn. The result of the desultory campaigning was a truce made in mid-September to last through the winter months until April 1258.

On 14 March 1258, even before the truce expired, the king was ordering his barons to appear at Chester on 24 June to invade Gwynedd. But for once, warfare was to be avoided. On 11 June, parliament met at Oxford, attended by many of the Marchers. Here the barons set out how they thought the kingdom should be run, for concern at Henry III's continued financial mis-management of the realm was reaching breaking point. In this, The Mad Parliament, the lords of Brecknock were at the forefront of the movement for reform which in effect placed the Crown under a permanent regency council. From the Welsh Marches, Earl Richard of Gloucester and Glamorgan, Earl Humphrey Bohun, Roger Mortimer of Wigmore, John fitz Geoffrey of Longtown, Peter Montfort and Hugh Dispenser were elected as some of the 12 baronial representatives who were in future to advise the king. Eleven further members of this council were nominated by the Crown. The new regency council made a truce with Llywelyn on 17 June, which was supposed to last until 1 August 1259. The terms of this stated that each party was to have seisin of the lands, men, castles and other things as they now lay. Although this treaty must in the long term have favoured the new government as it allowed them a breathing space to bring their power to bear on the problem, many saw it as a cowardly surrender. The resulting royalist backlash paralysed the council and immediately showed the weakness of any committee trying to run a kingdom. They disliked the king and the manner in which he ruled the kingdom, but they could not agree amongst themselves how to run it any better.

The initiative in Wales was left with Llewelyn who, on about 13 January 1259, held a meeting of the nobles of Wales in Arwystli. From there he marched with a large army southwards through his land of Gwrtheyrnion, captured from Roger Mortimer in December 1256, and into Buellt, where he once again granted the cantref to Maredudd ab Owain. However, by the spring, as soon as the army had gone, the province was recovered by Roger Mortimer, the chroniclers stating that 'it withdrew from Maredudd's protection.' Roger Mortimer then installed his own garrison in the castle on behalf of the Lord Edward, so excluding both Cantilupe and Bohun from this old Braose possession. Mortimer's campaign in the cantref would seem to have finished by 10 April when the constable of Bridgnorth Castle was ordered to receive all the malefactors sent to him by Roger Mortimer 'from those parts where he is preserving the king's peace.' Those parts were obviously Buellt.

Around Christmas 1259, Llywelyn again took possession of the cantref of Buellt, but once more the castle and town of Builth held out. On 10 January the king wrote from France making Roger Mortimer captain of the Welsh March in response to Llywelyn's breach of the truce. The Marchers ordered to be intendant on him included the familiar names of Reginald fitz Peter of Blaenllyfni, Humphrey Bohun of Brecon, and Walter Clifford of Cantref Selyf. Henry III followed up this order on 26 January with a command to postpone the parliament and 'take measures for the relief of the castle of Buellt and protection of the Marches as Llywelyn ap Gruffydd had come with an army and engines to besiege the castle of Buellt.' To halt this attack the regency council were to place 40 days supply in the castle and prepare to defend Brycheiniog and Gwent which were also under attack. On 29 January the king yet again ordered 'the libration to Roger Mortimer, or his known messenger, of 100 marks provided for him and granted by the council of the nobles who are of the king's council for his expenses in defending the March of Wales against the rebel Welsh whilst the king is in the parts of France.'

Mortimer proved successful in holding the castle in spite of the non-compliance of the government in sending him money. But on 17 July it was betrayed by three men set to man the castle wall at night, ostensibly out of ill will to a clerk or notary set in authority over them. Another factor, and no doubt far more important, seems to be the vast bribe the three were offered, though it should be realised that the garrison of Builth Wells Castle was not solely English. As a result of their treachery the castle was taken 'without so much as an arrow-shot, with such men and horses and arms and equipment as were in it.' Soon after the castle's fall Owain ap Maredudd, Roger Mortimer's princely baron of Elfael, did homage to Prince Llywelyn and paid him 300 marks for his son Madog's release from jail. It would seem that Madog had been part of the Builth Wells Castle garrison, possibly even its constable. Others in the garrison were not so lucky, for Archbishop Baldwin of Canterbury wrote to the bishop of Llandaff asking him to admonish Llywelyn for slaughtering them! Rhys Fychan of Dinefwr Castle then came and destroyed the castle 'to the ground' so that 'not a stone remained upon another.'

Meanwhile Roger Mortimer had returned to the London Parliament unaware of the disaster.

On 30 July it was recorded in parliament that 'Roger Mortimer had come by the king's special precept to the parliament at London, where it was announced to the king and him, that on 17 July the castle of Buellt, which was in his keeping by the bail of Edward the king's son, was taken by the Welsh enemies of the king.' The king with his son Edward in his presence at Westminster, then released Roger 'from whatever might be imputed against him by the taking of the said castle,' implying that they didn't consider Roger culpable for the fall of this strategic castle which he claimed as his own.

There now followed an abortive royal attempt to retake what remained of Builth Wells Castle and re-establish control in the area. On 1 August the king wrote to Earl Richard Clare ordering him to form an army at Shrewsbury on 8 September to retake Buellt with the aid of, amongst others, the familiar list of Earl Humphrey Bohun, Roger Mortimer of Wigmore, Humphrey Bohun Junior of

*Crickhowell Castle from a survey made at the
beginning of the 16th Century*

58

Brecon and Reginald fitz Peter of Blaenllyfni. A further army was ordered to form at Chester to simultaneously invade north Wales, whilst the bishop of Llandaff was admonished to excommunicate Llywelyn and his allies and induce them to surrender Builth Wells Castle and other lands in his diocese which had been taken against the terms of the truce. The truce with Llywelyn was in fact soon renewed, the king and his council finding themselves unable to agree on how best to pursue the war, whilst Roger Mortimer was compensated to the tune of 60 marks a year for the loss of his land.

On about 29 November a rebellion against Roger Mortimer took place in Maelienydd. As a consequence Mortimer and Humphrey Bohun Junior of Brecon came to Cefnllys with a Marcher army and encamped within the castle for a few days with the intention of rebuilding it. When Llywelyn heard of their plans, he advanced on Cefnllys and besieged the Marchers within the ruined castle walls, quickly forcing their retirement. Llewelyn followed up his advantage by marching into Breconshire taking the homage of many Welshmen. John Grey wrote to the king reporting that all the men of the Welsh tongue in the lordships of Humphrey Bohun of Brecon, Reginald fitz Peter of Blaenllyfni, Roger Picard of Tretower, Robert le Wafre of Pencelli, Robert Turbeville of Maescelyn/Crickhowell, Roger Tosny of Painscastle and those of many other great Marchers had gone over to the cause of Llywelyn.

Prince Llywelyn of Brycheiniog, 1263 to 1277
After the Cefnllys fiasco Humphrey Bohun Junior, who was still holding the castles of Brecon and Hay-on-Wye, even if most of the Welshmen of his barony had joined Llywelyn, was ordered to form an army at Hereford in early February 1263. A second army was formed at Ludlow, the clear intention being to retake the recently lost lands in Brycheiniog and Maelienydd. Due to dissension in the Marcher ranks, the king replaced Humphrey Bohun as commander of the southern army with John Grey.

After campaigning through Breconshire a Welsh army of 180 armoured horse and 10,000 foot was routed near Abergavenny. Despite this victory, on 5 March Peter Montfort wrote to the government saying that many of the Welsh communities of Brecknock were still adhering to Llywelyn, so he was remaining at

Abergavenny with 80 barded horse and between 3,000 and 4,000 foot soldiers. Soon afterwards, the Lord Edward, becoming ever more active in state affairs, appeared in the Marches with a force of Gascon mercenaries, and an Easter truce was arranged with Llywelyn. Edward then decided to remove the remains of the lordship of Brecon from the hands of the Bohuns. In early April he 'besieged' Hay and Huntington Castles and had Brecon surrendered to him together with all of the lands of Humphrey Bohun Junior. Edward then transferred all three castles with the province of Brycheiniog over to the custody of Roger Mortimer of Wigmore.

Edward then left the Middle March for the Perfeddwlad, taking John Grey with him and leaving Roger Mortimer as the main commander in Brecknock. Around this time Roger Mortimer was seriously wounded. Such a disaster must have seriously weakened his forces' already precarious hold on Brecknock, but not as much as the civil war that was about to break out in England.

On 25 May 1263 Henry III was issuing writs for the Marchers, including Earl Humphrey Bohun of Hereford, Reginald fitz Peter of Blaenllyfni, Walter Clifford, John Giffard, Roger Mortimer of Wigmore and Brecon, and Humphrey Bohun Junior the ex-lord of Brecon to march from Worcester on 1 August against the Welsh. In the meantime Llywelyn and his allies continued to put pressure on Brecknock. Early in June Brecon surrendered as the forces of Roger Mortimer were evicted from central Wales in great confusion. By 24 June, the simmering discontent within England finally erupted and the Barons' War began. To the complaints of financial mismanagement were added charges of arrogance against the Lord Edward and Roger Mortimer, including the way that they had deprived Humphrey Bohun of Brecon, only to lose it to the Welsh. It is therefore no surprise to find the Bohuns amongst the rebels who were soon at war with the royalist supporters, 'wasting one anothers' lands.' Campaigns in the summer ended with a parliament held at Winchester in October which sought to heal the rifts. There a new royalist Marcher party was born. It stayed in the forefront of national politics for the next few years and included Earl Humphrey Bohun Senior of Hereford, Roger Mortimer, who's troops still clung grimly to Hay-on-Wye and Huntington, the last Brecon lordship castles actually under English control, and Reginald fitz Peter the dispossessed lord of Blaenllyfni. This group soon came to be dominated by the personality of Roger Mortimer.

The barons continued to bicker over how the government should be run, many seeking a return to the Provisions of Oxford which had been formulated at the Mad Parliament of August 1258. To resolve the argument it was agreed to put the Provisions to the arbitration of King Louis of France. On 23 January 1264 Louis announced the result of his deliberations in the Mise of Amiens, finding totally in favour of King Henry III and against the reformist ideals of many of his baronage. Such a forthright condemnation of the Provisions of Oxford meant that full scale civil war was inevitable. In Breconshire Roger Mortimer and Earl Humphrey Bohun supported the king, whilst his son, Humphrey Junior, the dispossessed lord of Brecon, was an adherent of Earl Simon Montfort of Leicester, now the main leader of the reform movement.

Widespread fighting around the country culminated in the battle of Lewes, fought on 13 May 1264, where the royal army together with Roger Mortimer and his soldiers, who must have included many of the levies of Brecknock, met with the forces of the reformers under Earl Simon Montfort and Gilbert Clare, the young earl of Gloucester. After the battle, which proved a decisive royal defeat, many Marchers fled to Pevensey Castle on the Sussex coast where they were besieged by the victorious barons. Following a short and uneventful siege they were allowed to return home to the Marches, but only after they had agreed to give hostages and stand trial in parliament for their deeds. Both Henry III and the Lord Edward were captured.

On 14 May a safe conduct was issued to allow Roger Mortimer to return to his own lands, but on 31 May it was recorded that he had attacked the earl of Leicester's lands in the March in breach of of the truce arranged at Pevensey. The royalist Marchers gathered their forces under the leadership of Mortimer and Robert Turbeville of Crickhowell. In July Simon de Montfort's forces entered Hereford without opposition, and then proceeded to devastate the lands of Roger Mortimer. At Hay-on-Wye Castle, Roger Mortimer's constable, Walter Hackelutel, surrendered without resistance; the last stronghold of Roger Mortimer in present day

Breconshire had fallen to his enemies. Roger himself fell back to Wigmore Castle, whilst Earl Simon seized Richard's Castle and Ludlow. Roger retreated further to Montgomery where he was surrounded by Llywelyn in alliance with Earl Simon. On 25 August Roger surrendered his son William as a hostage for his good behaviour and was once again set at liberty to defend the Marches of Wales for the reformist government!

By early October Roger Mortimer had once more raised the standard of revolt and moved against Hereford and its strong city walls. With Roger were Robert Turbeville Senior of Crickhowell and John his brother of Rowlstone, marshal of the army, Hugh Turbeville and Miles Picard of Scethrog, who had earlier been bailiff of Haverfordwest for Humphrey Bohun Junior. For two days their forces battered the city defences, whilst the defenders launched regular sallies. When the news that a relief army was coming from London, Roger drew his forces off to Worcester to face the danger. There on 15 December he once more surrendered to Earl Simon at the Worcester Parliament. Despite this, many royalist Shropshire Marchers under Hamo Lestrange continued the war from their base at Montgomery Castle.

Throughout the winter of 1264/5 Roger Mortimer spent his time at Wigmore plotting and planning his vengeance as well as his return to Brecon. On 22 May 1265, he was instrumental in freeing the Lord Edward from his captivity in Hereford and bringing about a rapprochement between him and Earl Gilbert Clare of Gloucester. The royalist Marchers scented victory, for Earl Simon soon found himself surrounded at Hereford. Raising more troops from Archenfield, south-west Herefordshire, Earl Simon, taking Henry III with him, moved part of his army to Hay-on-Wye from where he carried on a dialogue with Prince Llywelyn, whilst the royalists besieged Gloucester. On 19 June 'at the castle near Pipton', Llywelyn agreed to peace terms with Henry III, who was nominally leading Earl Simon's army. By this agreement, which the king confirmed on 22 June, Llywelyn was to pay 30,000 marks at Whittington for recognition of his title of Prince of Wales. He also sent several thousand Welsh foot soldiers to the earl to help in his battles against the Marchers. Llywelyn's price for this help was clear, for in the treaty is the statement that the king will 'promise to aid him [Llywelyn] in the conquest of the rest of the lands and castles belonging to the right of the said prince and his magnates, which are in the hands of the common adversaries of the king and him and the king will grant to him the said lands and castles so conquered, especially the castle of Montgomery'!

Whilst the king and Earl Simon negotiated, the Lord Edward, Earl Gilbert of Gloucester, Roger Mortimer and the other Marchers were not idle. In turn the castles of Bristol, Monmouth, Usk, Newport, Brecon and Hay-on-Wye were reoccupied and very soon afterwards Llywelyn's 'new castle beyond Brecon' was thrown down. Much has been written about the identity of this castle and guesses for its identity have included Sennybridge and Camlais. Llywelyn had been in possession of Brycheiniog since December 1262, some 3 years before his 'new castle' was destroyed. After such a length of time building work could have been far advanced and therefore the castle might have been of some substance, but this cannot be proved.

What is especially interesting is the speed with which the Marcher allies re-occupied Brecon and Hay and the fact that Llywelyn thought it worthwhile to build yet another castle in this heavily castellated region. It would seem that the garrisons of the Brycheiniog castles must have switched sides; the cowardly surrender of Brecon to the Welsh in May 1263 followed by an equally quick submission to the Lord Edward under two years later suggests that the composition of the garrison did not change, merely their allegiance. This is an important factor when looking at the subsequent history of the Brecknock castles down to 1277.

Meanwhile, Earl Simon with his captive king had marched from Hay-on-Wye to Newport and back again to Hereford, but he could not escape the trap he was in with the Lord Edward and his loyal Marchers holding the valley of the River Severn against him. At the beginning of August he managed to cross the Severn at Kempsey, just south of Worcester, but was surrounded by Edward, Earl Gilbert Clare and Roger Mortimer and their allies at Evesham. There on the morning of 4 August 1265, the leading barons of the reformers, including Simon Montfort, were annihilated. Amongst the survivors of the massacre was Humphrey Bohun Junior, the one time lord of Brecon. He was taken, badly injured, to Beeston Castle in Cheshire and there, on 27 October, died of his wounds. His father, Earl Humphrey Bohun of Hereford, had kept to his royal allegiance and on 6 October he was at London reporting to the wounded and stunned King Henry III, 'that London had submitted to his instructions and had handed the city gate keys over to them.'

Even the victorious royalist barons desired some control over Henry, fearing yet further mismanagement. Consequently a power struggle now began between Roger Mortimer and the more moderate reformers led by Earl Gilbert Clare, who additionally did not wish to see his old friends crushed and reduced to penury. The first legal battle in this dispute went in favour of Gilbert: on 29 October 1265 custody of the honour and castle of Brecon was granted to him, during the minority of the 17 year old Humphrey Bohun, son and heir of the Humphrey who had just died at Beeston and grandson of the 'good' earl of Hereford. Gilbert obviously intended to return the lordship to its legal heir rather than support the claim of Roger Mortimer which, in April 1263, had helped fester the Barons' War.

Roger Mortimer, who had been made earl of Oxford on 27 October, was not the sort of man to take this lying down and Earl Gilbert probably knew it. Earl Humphrey Bohun remained in the favour of the new government, effectively now run by the Lord Edward, and on 30 April was granted custody of the castle of Usk and other lands beyond the Wye. On 21 February 1266 Robert Walerand was instructed to make a three year truce with Llywelyn, the Treaty of Pipton being repudiated on the grounds that the king was in captivity when it was signed, but nothing seems to have come of this initiative.

In the meantime Roger Mortimer had re-established himself at Hay-on-Wye Castle. On 4 May 1266 Roger was appointed 'to repress the king's enemies' and probably soon after this set out from Hay to retake the castle he still coveted at Brecon, despite any mandate claimed by Earl Gilbert Clare. On 15 May his forces were met by Llywelyn and his army was all but destroyed near Brecon, according to the Waverley chronicler, Roger almost alone surviving the slaughter of his troops, though this is probably an exaggeration. It is to be presumed that amongst his supporters at the battle would have been the Turbevilles of Crickhowell and the Wafres of

Pencelli, who had about this time married into the Mortimer family. Roger was probably not supported by the Picards as Roger Picard was probably still one of the barons 'disinherited' for having opposed Henry III. Indeed he may even have opposed Mortimer in the battle, lining his troops up on the side of Llywelyn!

By 24 June Roger headed east to support the Lord Edward and his brother Edmund who were besieging Simon Montfort's sons and their supporters in Kenilworth Castle. This siege became one of the most bloody and hard fought of the century—it was even said to be common for boulders flung by mangonels and trebuchets to collide and disintegrate in mid air. As the summer drew to an end starvation began to work its course amongst the garrison and Edward was persuaded by the more moderate of his supporters to offer a compromise in order to heal the wounds of the civil war. Compromise for the reformist barons was made easier by the fact that the reins of government could now be seen to be essentially in the hands of Edward and not Henry III. That compromise was reached on 31 October 1266 in the Dictum of Kenilworth, by which the lands of those disinherited after the battle of Evesham were to be returned to them for a suitable fine.

On 3 November this process was initiated for what remained of Brecon Lordship, still under the rule of Roger Mortimer. Roger was mandated to deliver the castles of Hay-on-Wye and Huntington with the manor of Kington over to Gilbert Clare who was to hold them during the minority of Humphrey Bohun, the grandson of the earl of Hereford, an order Roger complied with by the end of the year. At the same time the cantref of Buellt with its castle was granted to Edmund Plantagenet, Edward's younger brother, not that he had the slightest chance of retaking it from Llywelyn in the current circumstances.

Even with these 'peace gestures' towards the reformers and the surrender of the 1,200 man garrison of Kenilworth Castle on 20 December 1266, a lasting peace could still not be found. About 3 February 1267 Gilbert Clare withdrew to the Marches of Wales, made a pact with Llywelyn, and proceeded to make war against Roger Mortimer, citing partly as reason Roger's avowed opposition to the restoration of the disinheriteds' lands, and partly that Roger was still holding some of the territory awarded to his,

Gilbert's, custody. It is interesting to see Earl Gilbert allying with Llywelyn, whom in the long run was far more of a threat to him than Roger Mortimer.

On 21 February 1267 power was granted to Robert Walerand to make a truce with Llywelyn and the same day an inquisition was carried out on the Barony of Brecon at the king's command. This confirmed that the young Humphrey Bohun was the heir to the earldom of Hereford, Hay-on-Wye Castle, town and 'commote', Huntington Castle and borough, together with rents in Kington borough, Barton, New Kington, Moseleg, Chickwardine and Brilley. From this it is apparent that Brecon and the west of the lordship was still in the hands of Llywelyn. On 25 April 1267, Roger Mortimer was granted £217 5s 8d in compensation for the castles of Huntington and Hay.

On 28 August a parliament was held at Shrewsbury, partly in preparation for a new treaty with Llewelyn. This duly followed when, on 29 September, the Treaty of Montgomery was signed between the king and Llywelyn by which Llywelyn was recognised as Prince of Wales but agreed to return all those lands and rights he had occupied in times of war, with the exception of the lands of Brecon and Gwrtheyrnion which he had conquered. Llywelyn was also allowed to retain seisin and possession of the land of Buellt. Among the other terms, Roger Mortimer was allowed to build a castle in Maelienydd and once that was done, judgement was to be given over the land disputed between Roger and Llywelyn.

The crucial fact about the treaty remains the clause that Marcher law was to apply in the lands retained by Llywelyn beyond the limits of his principality—and that a commission was to determine such cases. What had been forgotten, or was conveniently ignored, was that Marcher law as such did not really exist. The Common Law of England existed as also did the law of Hywel Dda in Wales, but Marcher Law was instituted by various independent Marcher lords, through their own common customs. A Marcher lord acted as king in his capacity of lawgiver. How then could his law be applied when he had been expelled from his lands by Llywelyn? There would seem little doubt that Llywelyn regarded himself as the Marcher lord of Brecon, so his word there must have been law. It is doubtful if the Lord Edward, Humphrey Bohun or Roger Mortimer would have seen things in a similar light. However, for the time being the treaty was agreed and Llywelyn remained in seizin of the lordship of Brecon and most of its castles except for Huntington and Hay-on-Wye. The lordship of Blaenllyfni also seems to have remained in Llywelyn's hands. Its lord, Sir Reginald fitz Peter was one of the barons found some time later, on 14 March 1268, in the entourage of Roger Mortimer when he sold his right to the earldom of Oxford back to Robert Vere for 2,500 marks.

There were still problems to be sorted out between Llywelyn as lord of Brycheiniog and Gilbert Clare as the lord of the eastern part of Brecon lordship in the stead of his charge the young Humphrey Bohun. Goodwill on both sides led to a conference with royal commissioners at Montgomery on 14 September 1268 to discuss the demarcation lines to be drawn across Brecknock. This was followed on 27 September by a meeting of the earl and the prince at Pontum Monachorum in the lands of Dore Abbey in Cantref Selyf. It might also suggest that Bronllys Castle had survived Llywelyn's storm, or that John Giffard had bowed briefly to Llywelyn's will. At the bridge it was agreed that Llywelyn was allowed to retain the homage of the men of Senghennydd north of the Caeach and of the men of Miskin north of Pontypridd. This would indicate that Brecon was in the hands of Llywelyn as the Treaty of Montgomery states. It was further agreed that the parties would meet again soon after 6 January at Eadbryn in Brecon to settle any further disputes. Compromise and goodwill seemed the order of the day.

On 2 August 1270 the Lord Edward appointed Philip Basset, Roger Mortimer and Robert Walerand to act as the guardians of the kingdom for his father, Henry III, while he was away on Crusade. However, peace at home was not to last. That same August Humphrey Bohun became 21, was declared of age, and Gilbert Clare must have returned to him the remnants of his land of Brecon. It would also seem likely that he supplied the young Humphrey with troops to retake the other parts of his barony. As a consequence, on 16 October 1270 a commission was inaugurated concerning the aggressive excesses of Llywelyn, Earl Gilbert Clare and various unnamed Marchers. War would also seem to have continued in Glamorgan, and Llywelyn also began to become irregular in his payments to the Crown agreed under the Treaty of Montgomery four years previously. He acknowledged on 31 March 1271 that he was 3,000 marks in arrears. The slowing of payments and the beginning of further military operations were obviously interrelated.

In Brycheiniog the pressure of the Marchers was increasingly being felt. On 7 November 1271 Einion Sais ap Rhys of Brecon acknowledged the return of his hostage from Llywelyn, Prince of Wales and Lord of Snowdon, in return for his observance and fealty to him for ever. Einion promised Llywelyn that he would, if the prince so wished, return the hostage and that if he failed to do so or otherwise broke fealty, friends were bound by their word to pay 200 marks each to Llywelyn. The document was witnessed at Rhyd y Bryw, half way between Brecon and Llandovery and near, if not at, Sennybridge Castle itself. A similar notification was made by Meurig ap Llywelyn of Brecon. It is interesting to note that the two adherents of Llywelyn call themselves 'of Brecon' and it would seem that they were responsible for the defence of the town and castle. Certainly they appear nowhere in Norman records of the barony and when what followed is considered, it seems certain that these men were appointed by Llywelyn to guard his interests in Brycheiniog. In this they eventually proved unsuccessful.

The year 1272 saw Humphrey Bohun Junior again attacking Brycheiniog in a vain attempt to expel Llywelyn and his supporters. It would seem likely that Llywelyn wrote a letter of complaint about this attack to Edward, who was still on Crusade. Edward appears to have replied to his father, or more likely his regency council, for, on 30 October, Edward was informed that 'redress would be made for any violence used by the earl of Gloucester, Humphrey Bohun and other Marchers in attempting to regain Brecon and other Welsh lands.' Breaches of the truce by them and Llywelyn would be amended at the ford of Montgomery 'so it is not the king's fault if justice has not been done to the prince in these matters.' The implication is that the government would not interfere in the fighting in Brecknock as this was beyond their remit. Such an attitude was a *carte blanch*e for Humphrey to continue with his destabilising policy in central Wales. This, it can be assumed, he did with gusto, and Llywelyn may have encouraged counter raids towards Humphrey's base at Hay-on-Wye as it became more obvious that he would obtain no satisfaction at the ford of Montgomery!

The problems in Brycheiniog were probably exacerbated by the death of Henry III on 16 November. In the following January, the archbishop of York, Roger Mortimer and Robert Burnell convened a parliament to take oaths of fealty on behalf of the still absent Edward. One person who was conspicuous by his non-attendance was Llywelyn. Later, in justification of his absence, Llywelyn claimed that the advice of his vassals was that he would endanger his person by entering into the company of those who were attacking him and supporting his enemies. Presumably warfare continued in Brycheiniog, indeed on 18 May 1273 the regency council wrote to Llywelyn decrying his men having 'invaded Brycheiniog, the land of Humphrey Bohun, and other lands of his, laying them waste ... and having also presumed to besiege and occupy his castles.' The council, in the name of the king, commanded Llywelyn to desist in his warlike activities. In return they promised that any injuries inflicted on Llywelyn by Humphrey Bohun or other Marchers would receive full justice.

Later, on 13 September the council rebuked Reginald fitz Peter of Blaenllyfni and his vassal Hugh Turbeville of Crickhowell, for aiding Humphrey Bohun in his attack upon Brecon Castle against Llywelyn and the terms of the truce. This would tend to suggest that the final assault on Brecon came from the Usk rather than the Wye valley. The full story will never be known, but it is certain that by the end of the year Einion Sais and Meurig ap Llywelyn were ousted from the capital town of the barony.

On 26 February 1274 Llywelyn wrote from Criccieth in Gwynedd to the council stating that he was refusing to pay any more of his Montgomery fine of 1267 until the earl of Gloucester, Humphrey Bohun and the other Marchers had withdrawn from the lands they had illegally occupied. From this it was obvious that Llywelyn found himself unable to reverse the defeat he had suffered at Brecon. Probably in answer to this letter, on 24 April, Earl William Beauchamp of Warwick, Roger Clifford, John Giffard, the prior of St Thomas without Stafford, William Bagod and Odo Hodenet were ordered to go to Montgomery a month after

Easter and make a truce between Llywelyn and Humphrey Bohun of Brecon which was to last until 29 September. On 11 September 1275 Llywelyn wrote to the pope complaining that King Edward still retained the lands of certain Welsh barons pertaining to his principality even though they had been in Llywelyn's peaceful possession after 1267, (clearly alluding to Brecon amongst other places), and that Gruffydd ap Gwenwynwyn and Dafydd ap Gruffydd (Llywelyn's brother) who had recently plotted Llywelyn's death were maintained by the king and continuously attacked him, and that the king summoned him to pay homage in unsafe places.

On the Marcher side, Earl Humphrey Bohun of Hereford died on 24 September 1275 and was buried soon afterwards at Llanthony Secunda. His considerable wealth and possessions finally passed to his grandson Humphrey of Brecon and now earl of Hereford, who agreed to serve Edward I with 5 knights and 10 barded horses for the 'five fees' he claimed to owe for Brecon lordship. This was no doubt yet another signal for Bohun aggression in Brycheiniog. Early in 1276 Trahaearn ap Madog of Brecon came over to Humphrey. His son, in trying to do likewise, was captured by Prince Llywelyn and Trahaearn asked the king to intervene for his release. There could have been little now left of Llywelyn's power in the lordship.

On 26 April 1276 Llywelyn again defaulted in paying homage to the Crown and Edward put in motion his first war as king against the Welsh. On 24 June Llywelyn claimed that his lands were being attacked 'with a great multitude of horse and foot, with flags flying.' Bromfield had been invaded by Dafydd ap Gruffydd and the men of Chester and Shropshire; whilst Gruffydd ap Gwenwynwyn, the bishop of Hereford, Roger Mortimer and the earl of Hereford had attacked Llywelyn's possessions [no doubt Gwrtheyrnion, Buellt and the remnants of his power in Brycheiniog] from their lands; whilst further forces invaded the lands of Llywelyn's vassals and nephews, the sons of Rhys Fychan of Dinefwr, in South Wales. Rhys ap Gruffydd, the constable of Buellt, wrote to Llywelyn saying he had made a truce with Roger Mortimer to last until 1 August but that Roger had since despoiled the merchants of Buellt, Elfael, Gwrtheyrnion and Cardigan at Leominster and imprisoned some. Worse, there was little he could do to claim redress in the face of increasing hostility. On 15 July Llywelyn complained of this to Edward, stating that 122 merchants had been seized by Roger at Leominster and Montgomery and one slain. Llywelyn did not want war against Roger and his fellow Marchers, but in the current situation unless he had redress he would have no option.

On 16 November Roger Mortimer was appointed captain of Shropshire, Staffordshire and Herefordshire and ordered to bring Llywelyn and his adherents back to their royal allegiance. Roger does not seem to have been sluggish in this. According to the Welsh Chronicles, before the year 1276 was out, Powys had been gained for Gruffydd ap Gwenwynwyn, and Cedewain and Ceri, Gwrtheyrnion and Buellt for Roger Mortimer and the earl of Lincoln, and the earl of Hereford had won possession of Brycheiniog. How much reliance can be placed on this evidence when compared to the royal records is another matter, as fighting seems to have continued in the Middle Marches until the early summer of 1277.

Of the barons of Brecknock few details occur in the records. Roger Picard of Tretower was campaigning with the army of Henry Lacy at the siege of Dolforwyn Castle between 31 March and 8 April 1276. On 6 July protection was given until 29 September for Hugh Turbeville of Crickhowell going into Wales. Other forces were also forming to attack Llywelyn from the Middle Marches. On 16 August Roger Mortimer and Humphrey Bohun led 2,700 men for the king from Buellt, Brecon, Elfael, Maelienydd and Gwrtheyrnion; Buellt at this time being held by Hywel ap Meurig as constable and steward of the king. Interestingly, the captain of the Brecon contingent was Meurig ap Llywelyn, the very man who had sworn his loyalty to Llywelyn in 1271. Additional troops to the number of 400 foot came from Brycheiniog under Maredudd ap Rhys, Hywel ap Goronwy, Maredudd ap Llywelyn and Gruffydd ap Rhys—Llywelyn's rule in Brycheiniog was undoubtedly over. The Prince of Wales could not resist such force and was obliged to submit at Flint Castle on 23 August 1277. By the subsequent Treaty of Rhuddlan, signed on 9 November 1277, he accepted the limits of a much smaller principality. For Llywelyn ap Gruffydd, Brecon and the Middle March was forgotten, for the time being.

The last battles of Llywelyn, 1278 to 1282

With the peace treaty settled and the disputes in the Marches of Wales set before a panel of judges it might have been expected that things would have slowly sorted themselves out without further recourse to bloodshed. However that was not to be even though Roger Mortimer seemed resigned to his loss of Brecknock.

On 10 January, Rhys ap Maredudd of Dryslwyn, under the supervision of Payn Chaworth who was appointed justice for west Wales, was ordered to widen the passes in his domains for the security of the route from Carmarthen to Brecon. Similar instructions were sent to many others, including Humphrey Bohun of Brecon. On the same day the commission was established to look into the remaining legal disputes in the Marches and Wales.

Disputes over ownership of land and advowson of churches continued into 1281, whilst relationships between Llewelyn and the king gradually soured. On 21 March Llewelyn and his brother Dafydd rose in revolt. Edward made Roger Mortimer the captain of the army and put the whole community of Shropshire, Staffordshire and Herefordshire at his command, and ordered various barons, one of whom was Reginald fitz Peter of Blaenllyfni, to be under his orders. On 9 April, as the seriousness of the revolt was realized and fighting spread to the southern March of Carmarthen, the king ordered the newly rebuilt Builth Wells Castle to be provisioned for defence. Despite his firm support over the years for Henry III and his son, Edward, Roger Mortimer on this occasion seems to have been playing a duplicitous game, for the order to him on 15 October to cease supplying Llywelyn's needs does not seem to be the actions of the Roger Mortimer of old. By 17 June Builth Wells Castle was commanded by Roger Lestrange, no doubt under the auspices of Roger Mortimer, who between July and October 1282 was told to regard the land between Oswestry and Buellt as his theatre of operations.

In June 1282 Reginald fitz Peter of Blaenllyfni complained to the king that Grimbald Pauncefot, who had superseded Hugh Turbeville at Crickhowell, was refusing him his service of four barded horses which he owed for his mesne lordship. Reginald, undismayed by this act of virtual treachery in time of war, set off to join Earl Gilbert of Gloucester at Carmarthen. By 14 June Gilbert's army had been joined by Thomas fitz Walter Aubrey, the constable of Brecon Castle, and was camped at Llanddeusant, ten miles from Llandeilo. Gilbert clearly intended to settle his score with Llywelyn by an assault on Dinefwr Castle, the capital of the disintegrated principality of Deheubarth, but two days later the earl was defeated at the battle of Llandeilo. In the action William Valance Junior, the heir to Pembroke, was killed in a narrow defile and after the battle the remnants of Reginald fitz Peter's force of 10 barded horses and 300 footmen left the earl 'without leave'. Reginald, probably remembering what had happened to his Welsh lordship after the fiasco of Cefnllys back in 1262, was rushing home to protect his lands, the Welshries of which would no doubt have been heartened by his and the earl of Gloucester's defeat.

On 2 September 1282, £500 was consigned to be sent to Roger Mortimer from Chester 'to expedite certain special business of the king in those parts where up to the present... [text destroyed] ... And if ... he needs ... to take the said money to his lord, then the escort which he ...' and was sealed with the king's private seal. What 'special business of the king' Mortimer was seeing too is not known, but it seems likely that he was playing Llywelyn's game and aiding the prince surreptitiously in his war against King Edward. Through Gwladys Ddu, his mother, Roger and his sons had the blood of Llywelyn Fawr in their veins. Llywelyn ap Gruffyd had no sons, and now no wife, just a daughter, Gwenllian. He was also growing old and, like most Welsh princes, held his brothers generally in indifference or contempt. Would Llywelyn have wanted to see his principality escheat to the Crown on his death or his daughter married against his will by the king? Did he wish to see his brother Dafydd, who had plotted to kill him and done all in his power to bring him down, succeed him as Prince of Wales? Might not then his enemy of old, with whom he had been in friendly contact since the end of the last war, not make a better successor? Perhaps he could also provide Llywelyn with a suitable wife. The children of Matilda Clifford, the daughter of another of Llywelyn Fawr's daughters, were fast coming of age and although young, might well have given Llywelyn the son he must have yearned for. After all Roger had signed a pact of friendship with Llywelyn to aid him against all men, except for the king, and had not Roger already been helping him by sending him supplies to the king's annoyance? All these questions are unanswerable, but they may suggest that Roger and Llywelyn were laying a plot together, when fate once more intervened.

On 16 October 1282 Roger Mortimer died suddenly at the old Braose baildom of Kingsland, apparently of a cold. After his death and burial at Wigmore Abbey the monks wrote his epitaph:

> Here is buried, he who remained in glory
> Roger of the world, the second of Mortimer
> He who was great and was called Lord of Wigmore.
>
> While he lived, all Wales feared him
> All Wales was ground down in permanence by him
> They were all beaten by him in combat.

Soon after his death the king wrote to Roger's son, Roger of Chirk and Pencelli, and told him to 'so conduct himself against the king's Welsh enemies where his father was captain of the king's garrisons that the king, so far as lies in Roger's power, may seem to recover to some extent in the son what he has lost in the father. As often as the king ponders over the death of Roger's father he is disturbed and mourns the more his valour and fidelity, and his long and praiseworthy services to the late king and to him recur frequently and spontaneously to his memory.'

Meanwhile, Llywelyn moved into the lands of the dead Roger Mortimer where he planned once more to raise the Middle March to his banner.

At the end of November Roger Lestrange, who had lately been released from his charge of Builth Wells Castle which had been handed to John Giffard, informed the king that he would not imperil his Shropshire forces with a march over the mountains of Berwyn and Rug to engage the enemy; instead he would use his men in blockade, as many supplies were still reaching Llywelyn. He therefore asked that Roger Mortimer Junior should do the same at Chirk as should also the bailiffs of Buellt and Brecon, and Lady Matilda Mortimer at Radnor and her son Edmund in Maelienydd. Obviously Roger Lestrange was under no misapprehension as to who was supplying Llywelyn, though he appears not to have known why. On the very same night as this letter was written, Roger had word that Prince Llywelyn was on the move.

On 10 December 1282 Llywelyn moved from Powys into Roger Mortimer's land of Gwrtheyrnion with 160 cavalry and 7,000 foot to take the homage of the men there, at the deceitful request of Roger's sons according to the *Dunstable Chronicle*. He camped for the night near Abbey Cwmhir and while he was there all the potentates of the March assembled their forces against him. The next day Llywelyn set out for the south gaining possession of Buellt up to Llanganten. Then, according to the Welsh Chronicle, Llywelyn 'sent his men and his steward to receive the homage of the men of Brycheiniog, and the prince was left with but a few men with him.' In the afternoon of 11 December he appears to have split off from his remaining troops with a little band of 17 or 18 men to keep a rendezvous, but with whom is not recorded. He was intercepted at Aberedw, according to folklore, just down the Wye from Builth Wells; whilst the *Welsh Annals* state clearly that he was killed 'in battle' not far from Llanfair in Buellt. The *Annals of Chester*, agreeing with the elegy by Gruffydd ab yr Ynad Coch on Llywelyn's death, state simply that 'Llywelyn and a few followers were killed in the land of Buellt.' It seems most likely that the Marchers under Roger Lestrange and Roger Mortimer of Pencelli fell upon this little band and slaughtered them in an almost secret affair at dusk on Friday 11 December. Again according to the Welsh Chronicles, 'Roger Mortimer [of Chirk and Pencelli] and Gruffydd ap Gwenwynwyn, and with them the king's host, came upon them without warning; and then Llywelyn and his foremost men were slain.' The *Annals of Waverley*, which again were remarkably well informed about Welsh affairs, state simply that Llywelyn was captured by Edmund Mortimer and many Marchers and then beheaded before many Welshmen were killed by an assault or attack.

From this and other chronicles it can be deduced that the main Marcher army, after killing Llywelyn, moved against the now leaderless Welsh army and at 'a pre-arranged time', probably dawn the next day, fell upon them and inflicted a heavy slaughter. When the action was over, according to Roger Lestrange, 3,000 Welshmen and all the Welsh cavalry lay dead in the field and his own troops had suffered not one casualty! The *Dunstable Chronicle* states that over 2,000 Welshmen and all the cavalry were killed along with three of Llywelyn's magnates. The names of those who died in Llywelyn's last campaign are now, not surprisingly, largely lost, but the *Peterborough Chronicle* records that Almafan, lord of Lampadevar, Rhys ap Gruffydd the prince's seneschal, and Llywelyn Fychan of Bromfield were three lords amongst the slain on that fateful day.

Who actually killed Llywelyn is unknown, but some chronicles assigned the deed to Stephen Frankton, the 'centurion' of Ellesmere, though he seems to have gained little from the business. Others, like Robert Mannyng of Bourne, named Sir Robert Brody as the knight responsible for Llywelyn's beheading. Sir Robert certainly profited in the king's and Roger Lestrange's favour. In the margin of another contemporary manuscript now preserved in the British Library as *Cotton Nero Ms. D II, fo.182*, is a fine drawing of a man in mail armour kneeling with his hands clasped and awaiting a soldier behind him to strike off his head. So may have died Llywelyn, the one and only publicly recognised Prince of Wales.

John Peckham the archbishop of Canterbury had been at Pembridge in Herefordshire when Llywelyn was killed and he soon appeared at the scene and recorded that Llywelyn was the first of his army to be killed, 'in an ignominious death ... and his whole army was either killed or put to flight.' He too seems to believe that there was no battle, just a slaughter. On 17 December the archbishop wrote a letter to Bishop Robert of Bath and Wells about the affair with the proviso that he desired to protect the king against the plots of his enemies. Consequently he sent to the bishop, 'enclosed in this letter, a certain schedule, expressed in obscure words and fictitious names, a copy of which Edmund Mortimer has, and was found in the breeches of Llywelyn, formerly prince of Wales, together with his small seal, which the archbishop is causing to be kept safely for the king. From this schedule the bishop can sufficiently guess that certain magnates, neighbours of the Welsh, either Marchers or others, are not too loyal to the king, therefore let the king be warned unless he come to some danger.'

Private War, Private Gain, 1283 to 1399

The dispute concerning Sir Grimbald Pauncefot's refusal to accompany Reginald in the Llandeilo campaign of June 1282 seems to have rumbled on with Sir Grimbald using his favour with the king to great advantage. In December 1283, Reginald wrote an exasperated letter to Edward I concerning the things Grimbald had told his friend 'which are against right and truth.' Reginald also reported that 'his long stay in the March by the king's command has caused him to expend much more than he ought to have expended in order to do his service.' From this it can be discerned that there was still unrest in southern Brecknock and that the king thought it wise for Reginald to continue his military service there against Prince Dafydd ap Gruffydd's men. As late as 7 May 1283 John ap Dafydd of Arwystli had been sent south by the new prince as a leader of the Welsh of central Wales.

Probably around 7 December 1283 Reginald wrote again to the king complaining how Grimbald still withheld the service of four barded horses which he owed Reginald 'for the tenement which he holds of Reginald in Crickhowell' and which he had used in the king's service with Roger Mortimer in the vicinity of Montgomery during the war of 1282. In further correspondence Reginald noted that he had five times called out the men of Crickhowell to aid him in the war against Prince Dafydd and Rhys Fychan and on no occasion had they appeared. Also Grimbald had appeared before Reginald's court, but had defaulted on his pleas. Consequently Reginald asked that they should both be fined 100 marks by the king and that the king should keep the money of the loser, so sure was he of his right.

Grimbald Pauncefot also thought that he had a strong case. In March 1284, he reminded the king that the king himself had ordered him to send others in his stead to the command of the earl. This he had done and he requested the king's letter to that effect. He also complained of Reginald demanding his presence in his court even though he, Grimbald, was in the service of the king and therefore performing far more important tasks.

Whilst this case was being contested, Grimbald was in fact engaged in the fray against Prince Dafydd. On 26 April 1283, Earl William Valance of Pembroke wrote to him or his lieutenant

demanding that he send to Castell y Bere, which had just surrendered to him, corn, flour, bacon, malt and honey. Obviously he
thought Grimbald well positioned to supply him from his land of
Ystrad Yw Isaf. However, there was also a threatening note
attached to the demand, that if the bearer, John Knoville, was not
supplied these victuals by Grimbald, Valance had on the king's
behalf granted him the power 'to take the said victuals wherever
they can be found, and to send them to the castle'! This tends to
give the impression that Grimbald might have been seen by Valance
as a bit of a slippery customer!

Meanwhile, Reginald fitz Peter seems to have been busy
pillaging the lands of the Prior of Brecon, as towards the end of
July 1283 Archbishop Peckham of Canterbury wrote to him
complaining of his actions. Obviously this did not prove
successful for on 1 August 1284 the archbishop had to renew his
complaint. Reginald fitz Peter, at least 61 years old, died shortly
before 5 May 1286, and was succeeded by his son, John fitz
Reginald. The son does not appear to have been an overly

*The remains of the hall at Brecon Castle seen from across the Usk
as depicted in 1805*

pleasant person. Sometime after 1304 the sheriff of Glamorgan, probably at John's request, seized William Hayworth, a clerk, 'for a long time the mortal enemy' of John. The sheriff handed William over to John who, without a court judgement, hung him on a gibbet by the roadway over night. The next morning he was found to be still alive and Sir John ordered two strips to be flayed from his thighs, from his breeches to his heels, and then hung him up again. He was found still alive on the second day and this time Sir John ordered four strips to be taken from his skin and salt rubbed into the wounds. William was then hung back up and died soon afterwards. William's widow, Marjorie, claimed retribution against Sir John and the court acknowledged her petition with an endorsement allowing an appeal. What came of the case is not recorded, but Blaenllyfni was seized on the death of Sir John in 1310 and passed into the hands of Roger Mortimer of neighbouring Pencelli to the exclusion of John's son and heir Herbert. Perhaps William Hayworth did gain some small measure of retribution in death.

In 1287 war had once more come to Brecknock, when Rhys ap Maredudd, the lord of Dryslwyn, rebelled against what he saw as the perfidy of Edward I in both refusing him land to which he thought himself entitled and interfering with the running of the lands that he did hold. As a result, in early June he started a general war against the king in Deheubarth and this spread into Brecknock and Glamorgan. In July Earl Gilbert Clare was appointed 'captain of the parts of Brecknock.' Once more it was Gilbert's job to control the Welsh of Deheubarth and in August the feudal might of England, including 400 of Roger Mortimer's foot soldiers, marched on Dryslwyn Castle, besieged it, undermined its walls and captured the fortress and town. Rhys struck back on 2 November, storming Newcastle Emlyn. As a result, Thomas fitz Walter Aubrey, the constable of Brecon, wrote to his lord, Humphrey Bohun, telling him of the events and reporting that 'the earl's castle and town of Brecon are in good state and will be well defended.' In the meantime opportunity was taken for a private vendetta by the Welsh of Brecon Lordship against their neighbours of Buellt. Such animosities were all too common in medieval Wales.

In 1289 Earl Humphrey went to war as lord of Brecon against his rival and one time friend, the earl of Gloucester, over the southern boundaries of his lordship. This was to be the last private war launched in Wales against the express wishes of the king. The first shot in this feud was fired on 28 June 1289, when the king ordered Earl Gilbert to stop building his new castle of Morlais on the lands of the earl of Hereford in Brycheiniog. This would seem to have signalled a general war between the two barons—skirmishes were fought, townships harried, flocks and herds driven off, even a church, probably Vaynor, was desecrated by Gloucester's seneshal. The king's order for the disturbances to cease was ignored, but on 18 January 1290 an enquiry was ordered into the attack made upon Humphrey Bohun and his men of Brycheiniog by Gilbert Clare and his men of Morgannwg.

The trouble rumbled on until the parliament of Abergavenny on 20 October 1291. As a result of the findings of this body on 19 February 1292, Humphrey's honour of Brecknock was confiscated by the king for his wilful continuation of the war against the royal mandate. Both Brecknock and Glamorgan thereby came into the hands of Roger Burghill, no doubt a descendant of the Burghills who had for so long served the lords of Brecknock. For his contempt of the royal mandate, Humphrey was fined 1,000 marks, a pittance against the 10,000 mark fine of Earl Gilbert who was considered the aggressor. Gloucester was also ordered to pay Hereford the sum of £100 for the damages he had inflicted on the land of Brecknock. The only lasting significance of this war was the foundation of Morlais Castle by Earl Gilbert which was probably meant to overshadow Earl Humphrey's comparatively puny castle at Vaynor.

The Clare-Bohun dispute of 1289-91 possibly weakened English control in Wales, for in 1294 another great revolt blew up under the leadership of Madog ap Llywelyn, the descendant of a prince of Meirionydd vanquished by Prince Llywelyn in 1256. In south Wales the descendants of the Lord Rhys once more rose in revolt and war came again to Brecknock. The Welsh of Glamorgan under Rhys ap Morgan ap Maredudd of Caerleon attacked and destroyed the castles of Morlais and Cefnllys before King Edward marched against them and re-took Morlais, passing it into the care of Walter Hackelutel. The damage to Brecknock seems to have been considerable and the prior of Llanthony claimed that the collection of the tax of 1294-5 'was prevented by the notorious war between the king and the Welsh' in the archdeaconries of St David's and Brecon. Builth Wells Castle was attacked during the uprising and John Giffard was allowed his expenses in repairing the castle during 1297.

On 7 June 1295 King Edward, after leaving Drysllwyn Castle, wrote to his brother Edmund that all the men of the counties of Cardigan, Carmarthen, Ystrad Tywi and Buellt had come to the king's peace, but those of Brycheiniog and Glamorgan had yet to do so, though the king had been informed that they would do so shortly as their leader, Morgan ap Maredudd of Caerleon and Llandovery, had already submitted to him. He was also led to believe that Madog ap Llywelyn of Meirionydd and Maelgwn of Deheubarth would soon be in his power or dealt with 'in some other way'. He marched to Brecon on the 16th and Builth Wells on the 17th.

On 7 December 1295 Gilbert Clare died at Monmouth Castle, aged 52. He was followed not long afterwards by Humphrey Bohun who died in 1298, aged 50. Yet another of the leading players to die around this period was Sir Grimbald Pauncefot. His widow, Sibyl Turberville (d.1326), founded a new church in Crickhowell which is now the Church of St Edmunds, replacing the town's use of the ancient church of Llangadock and the baptismal chapel of St Mary at Maescelyn.

Tretower Castle from a survey made at the beginning of the 16th century

In 1297 war again broke out with France and in July Edward I called on John fitz Reginald of Talgarth to supply 50 men, John Giffard of Buellt and Cantref Selyf 100, William

Pederton Justice of West Wales 2,000, the aging Roger Picard, who would have been around 70 by now, 50 from Tretower and Gilbert Bohun 50 from Crickhowell to appear, ready for service overseas, at Hereford on 1 August. The Welsh who went with the Marchers were led by the dispossessed Welsh lords of the war of 1295 and were described disparagingly — 'Their weapons were bows, arrows and swords. They also had javelins and wore linen clothing and never wore armour.'

Roger Picard probably died during this campaign, for in 1297 his son John was recorded as lord of Ystrad Yw in the cantref of Talgarth. John himself died in 1306 and Tretower then passed to his sister Amicia in 1308, on the death of John's young son, Roger. Amicia had married Ralph Bluet of Raglan and the lordship passed through her to this ancient Marcher family. With this transfer Tretower Castle passed into obscurity, the Bluets far preferring their ancestral seat at Raglan in Gwent to Tretower. They may also have started the manor house which later became Tretower Court.

The services that the men of Buellt had done in Edward's campaigns in France and Scotland may have led to a change of attitude by the king, and when John Giffard died he again set one of their own over them when, on 22 June 1299, Philip ap Hywel ap Meurig was granted the cantref of Buellt for five years for a rent of £113 6s 8d. He was still holding it on 10 February 1315 when he was ordered to send £50 of his rent over to Roger Mortimer who was serving the new king, Edward II, in Gascony.

The new lord of Brecon, another Humphrey Bohun, was often in service in Scotland, taking part in the siege of Caerlaverock Castle in July 1300 and being captured after Bannockburn in 1314. In Wales a revolt blew up at the start of 1316 and on 11 February Humphrey was appointed captain of all the forces combined against Llywelyn Bren ap Rhys who was operating from Glamorgan. The war proved short-lived. As a result of his commission the earl invaded Morgannwg as best he could 'due to the state of the country and the season of the year.' The results were successful and on 22 March the earl wrote to the king reporting 'that he and his Mortimer neighbours have been in the most distant region of Morgannwg and achieved what they could ... as a result of which Llywelyn ap Gruffydd [a mistake for Rhys] and his two sons, and others, came to them at Ystradfellte and came to his peace and will, and are now in the writers custody in his castle of Brecon.' So ended the career of Llywelyn Bren who was soon afterwards executed, as apparently did the occupation of Castell Coch at Ystradfellte, where Llywelyn probably surrendered to Humphrey.

This was not to be Humphrey's last military triumph. Llywelyn Bren was said to have risen mainly against the oppression of the Dispensers of Glamorgan. His hatred of the Glamorgan upstarts was not singular and Edward II was soon forced to banish the Dispensers. Towards the end of 1321 they were back in the country and civil war ensued. Humphrey Bohun assisted the rebel barons in taking Gloucester, Newport, Cardiff and Bridgnorth, but thereafter the war did not go their way. The Mortimers were tricked into surrendering to the king on 13 January 1322, and on 16 March, Humphrey Bohun was killed at the battle of Boroughbridge when trying to force the bridge. 'For when the earl of Hereford, with his standard-bearer leading the advance, to wit, Sir Ralph Applinsdene, and Sir Roger Clifford and some other knights, had entered upon the bridge before the others as bold as lions, charging fiercely upon the enemy, pikes were thrust at the earl from all sides; he fell immediately, and was killed with his standard-bearer and the knights aforesaid ... but Sir Roger Clifford, though grievously wounded with pikes and arrows, and driven back, escaped with difficulty along with the others.' So fell yet another lord of Brecon in battle with his foes.

As a result of this action all of Brecknock that had not previously fallen into the king's hands did so now and the king set his own appointees in charge of the castles and ordered them to undertake inventories. Robert Morby was made the keeper of the castles (probably Brecon and Hay-on-Wye), town and land of Brycheiniog at 4s a day. William Werdale was made keeper of the castles and lands of Bwlch y Dinas, Blaenllyfni and Pencelli at 18d a day; Benedict Normanton of the castle and town of Bronllys and of the lands of Cantref Selyf at 2d a day; William Kaythorp of the castle, town and lands of Crickhowell and Ystrad Yw which had previously belonged to Aymery Pauncefot at 18d a day and Thomas Brayton was keeper of the castles, town and lands of Buellt at 2s a day. Rhys ap Hywel of Bronllys Castle was thrown into prison where he had to languish until the return of Roger Mortimer. Soon after these arrangements were made the king transferred the lands of Humphrey Bohun, the Mortimers, Rhys ap Hywel and Aymery Pauncefot into the hands of one Rhys ap Gruffydd who was still holding them at Michaelmas 1325.

The power of the lordship of Brecon was again displayed in late September 1326 when, in rebellion, Roger Mortimer of Wigmore returned from France with Isabella, the estranged queen of Edward II, Prince Edward and Earl Edmund of Kent and 700 mercenary Hainaulters. King Edward II fell back towards Wales and ordered Rhys ap Gruffydd on 11 October to bring to him as soon as he could at Gloucester 'such men-at-arms, hobelars and infantry as he could possibly gather to serve at the king's wages.' Rhys, who had custody of much of Breconshire spent £259 2s 8d over 8 days in raising his troops at Brecon. However he got no further. The rebel army dispersed the king's disintegrating forces which were supposed to form at Gloucester and Roger Mortimer himself called to his rebellion the troops of Brecon, Maelienydd, Gwrtheyrnion, Ceri and Cedewain and they flocked to his standard to the alleged tune of 10,000 men. Mortimer and his burgeoning troops chased the king and his shrinking retinue through Glamorgan where, on 16 November at Neath, Edward II was captured by, amongst others, Rhys of Bronllys Castle, the son of Hywel ap Meurig of Radnorshire.

After this rebellion Roger Mortimer of Wigmore, once more possessed of northern Radnorshire and large parts of Brecon, ruled England and Wales as regent and lover of Edward II's queen. The unfortunate and tyrannical Edward II met an unpleasant end at Mortimer's orders in the dungeon of Berkeley Castle, allegedly by having a red hot poker inserted in his rear. Despite his great triumph Mortimer could not hold back the jealousy of other nobles and his greed for lands earned him the nickname from his own son as the King of Fools. He was captured on the orders of his young suzerain, Edward III, at Nottingham Castle in 1330, tried at London and taken to Tyburn where he was hung.

Roger Mortimer of Chirk, Pencelli and Blaenllyfni did not live to see the triumph of his nephew of Wigmore. He had died in custody on 30 August 1326 just before his relative's victory. Roger Mortimer of Wigmore then seized his uncle's lands for himself, ignoring Roger of Chirk's son and heir, another Roger. This Roger survived until October 1333 when he died young, leaving a widow Juliane and a young son John who claimed his grandfather's barony from the king. The new king replied that 'neither the king or the council are advised yet to ordain remedy in this case because of the tender age of the child.' John was still alive on 31 August 1359, but he failed to regain any of his lands from his cousin, Earl Roger Mortimer of March.

The rest of the 14th century passed off with little military activity and the castles of Brecknock were allowed gently to decay, as the few remaining surveys of the castles indicate. The increase in documents does however shed some little light upon the foundation of one castle in the Marches of Brecon. On 3 February 1358 an inquisition found that Hywel Fychan ap Hywel, the grandson of Einion Sais of Penpont, 'was given a settlement of property ... between the Camlais Fychan and Camlais Fawr in the parish of Defynnog ... that which land and tenements the Lord Humphrey Bohun, once earl of Hereford and lord of Brecon, had given (*emit*) to lord Trahaearn ap Hywel for the purpose of strengthening the castle of Camlais.' Here is testimony that Camlais Castle probably existed before the death of Earl Humphrey in 1275 and that Earl Humphrey had asked Trahaearn ap Hywel, who in 1258 was serving Prince Llywelyn, to strengthen the castle. The question as to whether Humphrey granted the lands around Camlais Castle to Trahaearn before or after the Welsh War is unknown and probably unknowable. It is also possible that Camlais Castle had been built by Trahaearn or Llywelyn his suzerain, and then re-taken by Humphrey or his son some time before 1275. In addition it has to be remembered that these inquisitions took evidence from oral traditions which may not have been trustworthy; one Humphrey Bohun could easily be mis-remembered for another. The net result of this is that Camlais may have been the new castle of Llywelyn above Brecon thrown down by Prince Edward in 1265, and when the area was retaken in the war of 1276 a new Humphrey Bohun granted the ruined castle to Trahaearn together with extensive lands to ensure his loyalty to his new suzerain as well as to furnish for the castle's repair. Such arguments are of course circular without further information.

Buellt Castle and cantref passed through a variety of hands including the Lacys, Mortimers, Queen Isabella and Ebulo Lestrange, before being confirmed as being held by the Black Prince by grant of his father, King Edward III. Whilst Humphrey Bohun failed in his attempt of 1345-7 to gain control of Buellt, he did succeed in ousting Philip ap Rhys ap Meurig from the old Clifford castle of Bronllys. In 1347 Humphrey attempted to raise the troops of Cantref Selyf at the king's order, but Philip ap Rhys naturally claimed that right as his own. The quarrel was patched up, but in 1349 Humphrey brought an action of Quo Warranto against Philip, asking by what right he wielded his extensive Marcher powers at Bronllys Castle, arguing that only an earl or 'lord of an honour' could hold the quasi-regal marcher powers that Philip claimed. The king's court agreed with him and Philip was forced to swap Bronllys Castle and Cantref Selyf with Humphrey in exchange for lands at Shifnal in Shropshire. So ended the mesne barony of Cantref Selyf, formed in the emergency of 1144.

The last Humphrey Bohun died on 16 January 1373 and his castles in the Marches—Brecon, Hay-on-Wye, Huntington, Caldicot and Newton were seized by the crown before being granted to Thomas of Woodstock who had married Eleanor Bohun. On Thomas' execution for alleged treason the lordship of Brecon then passed via Eleanor's youngest sister, Mary, to Duke Henry of Lancaster. When Henry moved westwards against King Richard II the castles of Brecon and Hay-on-Wye were rapidly installed with scratch garrisons to defend them 'against the malice of King Richard and the lord's enemies coming from Ireland.' At the same time troops were sent from the lordship to reinforce the usurper who had advanced as far as Gloucester. Thankfully no fighting occurred in the province, Richard's capture occurring in the north of Wales. Henry then took the crown as Henry IV.

The Glyndwr Rebellion, 1400 to 1415
The Glyndwr rebellion initially had little effect upon the county of Brecon, although from as early as May 1401 reports began to

circulate of robbers and malefactors in the shire and defections to the rebels of entire communities in Buellt. In October 1401, for the first time in nearly 80 years, a serious military garrison was placed in the castles of Brecon and Builth Wells, 20 men-at-arms and 40 archers in each. Early the next year, on 12 June 1402, a Marcher army under Edmund Mortimer was destroyed by Glyndwr at Pilleth, to the west of Knighton. Soon afterwards, on 26 July 1402, a new military command was set up under Lord Richard Grey of Codnor which stretched from Cardigan to Brecon. This commission was expanded on 30 September when he was appointed king's lieutenant from Aberystwyth to Hay-on-Wye and ordered to form a force of 750 men for 3 months and establish himself in Brecon Castle with 40 men at arms and 200 English archers. At the same time the disaffected inhabitants of Brycheiniog were ordered to contribute a 'war loan' of £210 to Lord Grey above their normal taxation! Despite this, by 24 June 1403 Glyndwr's forces were laying siege to Brecon itself, a siege lifted by John Bodenham, sheriff of Herefordshire. Bodenham was able to write to the king on 7 July: 'On the Sunday last [1 July] ... we were at Brecon and broke the siege; and there were killed ... the number of 240 and upwards.'

Matters became worse for Henry when Glyndwr was joined in revolt by the Percys of Northumberland, who felt that their support of the usurper and subsequent service on his behalf in Scotland was not sufficiently well rewarded. The Earl of Norhumberland's son, Harry Hotspur, raised the flag of revolt in Cheshire which had had deep loyalty to Richard II. Henry IV heard the news whilst he was on his way north to actually join the Earl of Northumberland in a campaign against the Scots, and instead marched his army to Shrewsbury where he quickly brought Hotspur to battle and defeat on 21 July 1403. Henry subsequently brought his army to Brecon before marching on to retake Carmarthen Castle. On 8 September 1403 the king committed Painscastle and Clyro (Royle) to the earl of Warwick, Huntington to Countess Ann of Stafford, Crickhowell to John Pauncefot and Tretower to James Berkeley. The castles were to be 'furnished with fencible men, victuals, armour, artillery and all things needful ... that no damage or peril shall arise.' This order did not mention Hay-on-Wye Castle which on 30 October 1461 was described as ruinous having been destroyed by the Welsh rebels. Nevertheless a garrison was recorded in the castle in 1404. On 15 September 1403 the king was at Defynnog west of Brecon where he issued a mandate to Sir John Oldcastle of Herefordshire and others empowering them to receive into the king's peace the Welsh rebels of Brecknock, Buellt, Cantref Selyf, Hay-on-Wye, Glynbough and Bwlch y Dinas, on condition that they lay down their arms and took an oath of fealty. During the entire year the English presence north of Brecon in central Wales was reduced to solely the isolated garrison at Builth Wells Castle.

With Henry's retiral from Wales in 1403, Earl Richard Beauchamp of Warwick was appointed to command the fortress of Brecon. In February 1404 supplies sent to Brecon Castle included 6 cannon, 20lbs of gunpowder, 10lbs of sulphur, 20lbs of saltpetre, 42 breast plates and 12 basinets. At the same time the rebel communities west of Brecon Castle tried to make their peace with the king. They agreed to pay him 100 marks in 10 weekly installments to be re-admitted to his peace, but there were conditions attached—the king would have to suppress the revolt in Glamorgan before May for otherwise the men of Brycheiniog would find it impossible to reside in the king's peace. This is a stark assessment of one reason why the revolt proved so successful; it was impossible for one group of Welshmen to act without the consent of their neighbours if these neighbours had sufficient power to intervene.

In February 1405, John Bedell of Hay-on-Wye was granted the lands of 8 rebels who had forfeited their tenements in Hay-on-Wye and Bronllys. Two months later it was recorded that in Brecon there was a garrison of 40 lances and 240 archers, while in Hay Castle were 16 lances and 80 archers. These and other castle garrisons were now used as flying columns by Prince Henry and his commanders, combining their strengths to great effect. In March 1405 troops from the Brecon garrisons were used at the decisive battle of Grosmont— the tide had turned. By 1408 the county was beginning to revert one more to a more normal state and taxes were again being raised from the decimated countryside of a once prosperous land.

At the end of the 14th century the lordship of Brecon had raised over £1,500 per annum, by 1403 nothing could be raised, and by

1409, with the revolt well on the wane, it had only recovered to a mere £364. The scale of devastation and loss is obvious.

In September 1413 the new king, Henry V, demanded £1,200 from his lordship of Brecon, partly as a welcoming gift and partly in recompense for their late rebellion! This was not the end of the taxation for by 1420 (discounting the figures for 1419), over £5,700 had passed into royal coffers from the lordships of Brecon and Kidwelly. Such taxation did not mean disloyalty, for at Agincourt one of the victorious combatants was Dafydd Gam, who had for so long upheld the Lancastrian cause against Glyndwr at Brecon. Despite this, as late as 1416-18 garrisons were retained in the castles of Brecon and Hay-on-Wye where 14 and six men were paid for their services respectively. These precautions were probably taken against Sir John Oldcastle, now Lord Cobham after his marriage into the aristocracy, who had refused to renounce his support for Lollardism. After a trial at which Henry V had tried to save his old colleague in the wars with Glyndwr, Oldcastle had been declared guilty of heresy and imprisoned in the Tower of London, from which he had escaped. After an abortive Lollard rising in London, which had easily been dispersed, Oldcastle had escaped to Herefordshire and the Welsh borders with its known Lollard sympathies. In the end he was captured near Broniarth and put to death in London.

Decay and the Civil War 1416 to 1645

Henry, the second Duke of Buckingham, was lord of Brecknock in 1483 when he rebelled against the newly crowned Richard III. His accomplice in this revolt was Bishop John Morton of Ely who had been entrusted to Henry's care and incarcerated by him in the tower of his keep at Brecon. From that day forth this structure has been known as Ely's Tower. Henry formed an army at Brecon and marched eastwards to try to win the Crown, advancing into the Forest of Dean but failing to cross the River Severn because of unusual floods. Henry then fell back on Weobley Castle where his forces disintegrated through lack of pay and low morale. Henry himself was captured and executed on 2 November at Salisbury, after once again proving how important good weather was to a rebellion. Henry's son, Edward the third Duke of Buckingham, was born in Brecon Castle in February 1478, and met his own end in 1521 when he fell foul of King Henry VIII, perhaps after rashly boasting of his own royal connections.

The English Civil War of 1642 to 1648 saw little action in the county of Brecknock. At the beginning of the war, Herbert Price MP was sent by the king to raise regiments from the county, where-after Welsh troops were used extensively in the king's campaigns. A small garrison was also placed in Brecon Castle, but by 23 November 1645 the townspeople, fed up with supporting a losing cause, had destroyed the castle and the town defences to ensure that they would not be besieged by a victorious Parliament. So ended the military history of Brecon and its castles.

Brecon Castle

Masonry motte and bailey
Location: Brecon town centre (SO 044 286)
Access: Private. The Castle Hotel occupies the site of the
southern and part of the northern baileys. The motte and keep lie
in the private grounds of the bishop of Brecon

Flint tools dating from around 3000 BC have been found on the site, whilst the hill-fort to the east of the castle probably dates to around 400 BC and may still have been occupied when the Romans built their fort two miles west of the castle at Y Gaer between 80 and 100 AD.

The building of Brecon Castle began sometime before 17 April 1093 and from the first seems to have incorporated a town defence, both being completed after the defeat and death of King Rhys ap Tewdwr of Deheubarth who was probably killed where the high altar of the cathedral, once St John's Priory, now stands. The early town development incorporated the grounds of the Priory.

The castle may have been attacked in 1168 by Rhys ap Gruffydd, and was definitely occupied by royal forces in 1208. In 1215 the two remaining Braose brothers retook the castle in their struggle with King John and in 1217 the townsmen and Braose garrison successfully bought off Llywelyn Fawr. Llywelyn returned in 1231 and 1233, but did not succeed in taking the castle, though on both occasions the town was burnt 'and walls were thrown to the ground'. In early 1263 the castle was transferred to the keeping of Roger Mortimer of Wigmore. Mortimer seems to have immediately suffered problems of loyalty and as a consequence it appears he wrote to the king concerning Brecon Castle. The letter has survived but it is badly damaged and much of the parchment has been torn away. Nevertheless, its gist seems to be that Roger had been told by the Lord Edward (the future Edward I) to report any problems in Brecknock to the king if he could not reach Edward himself: '... the bailiffs of the earl of Hereford at Brecon distrain ... the men of his lord [Edward] grievously, because they do not come to carry his timber to the castle of Brecon, a thing which neither they nor their ancestors had ever done, or ought to do.' A little while later Roger was wounded in battle and his garrison 'shamefully surrendered' to Llywelyn about the end of May. An apparently successful attempt was made to regain the castle by the Lord Edward in June/July 1265, though the castle changed hands yet again soon after. The castle was then garrisoned by Llywelyn's supporters and in 1266 Mortimer tried to retake it, but was decisively defeated outside the town on 15 May. Prince Llywelyn then spent some considerable effort ensuring the safety of the castle; nevertheless it may have changed hands three times in 1273, with Humphrey Bohun Junior finally obtaining control. The castle may have been attacked by the Welsh in 1295 and

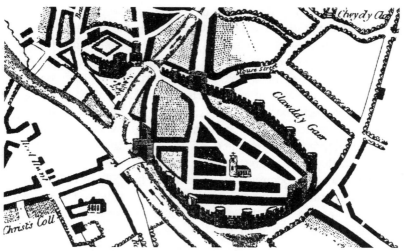

From surveyor Meredith Jones' plan of 1744

92

was a mustering point for the Bohun rebels against Edward II and the Despensers in 1321, falling undefended to royalist forces soon afterwards. A considerable amount of money was spent repairing the castle between 1400 and 1402, before it was besieged in 1403 by supporters of Owain Glyndwr, a siege broken by a relieving force under the command of the sheriff of Hereford. In 1483 the castle became the muster point for yet another abortive rebellion, this time by the Duke of Buckingham. The castle suffered from a fire in the 1490s, such that it was neglected by 1498. Nevertheless, following the Act of Union between England and Wales and the formation of the Council of the Marches of Wales, the castle was still able to host the King's Court. Indeed, the Great Hall was still usable in the early 17th century.

By the 13th century the castle was entered either from the main gate to the west, which was protected by a great portcullis, or from the east across the River Honddu where the present bridge stands. There was also a postern gate somewhere in the perimeter. Of these and the other encircling defences little or nothing now remains.

The main remaining defensive feature of the castle is the great motte, about 15 metres high and surmounted by the remnants of a shell keep, now known as Ely's tower. The keep's internal dimensions are 24m east to west by between 17m and 20m north to south. Inside this, judging by Meredith Jones' plan of 1744, was a large round tower similar to the one at Tretower Castle. This tower is less obvious in the drawings made by Speed in 1610 to accompany his maps of Breconshire and of Wales. If Jones' plan is correct, this round tower was probably the original Ely's Tower. Much of the shell keep has been disturbed by later landscaping which may also have involved the addition of the rampart running up the motte from the west. Building stone and good-quality mortar were found here when it was dug into in the 1950s. The shell keep appears to have consisted of several lengths of wall measuring some 5m long externally and forming a decagonal or dodecagonal enclosure. The main remaining feature of the masonry is a small projecting turret which has a deeply spurred base and old red sandstone quoins. The rest of the untidy, rubble-built walls are of local grey sandstone. Internally, the turret houses a small barrel-vaulted room with a small light to the east, possibly a bedroom.

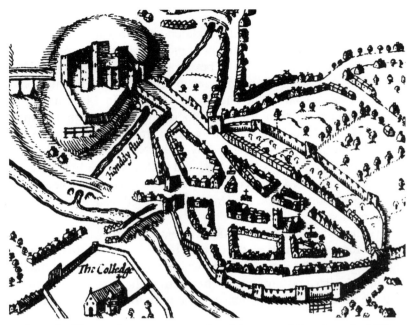

Speed's illustration accompanying his map of Brecknock, 1611

From the turret one wall continues to the north, while four sections of wall are still traceable running south and then east. These walls have at least 2m high plinths, stepped at the bottom on the south front. Stepped plinths tend to be of an early date, likewise there are no string courses in the turret which again suggests an early date, though, with its sandstone quoins, it may have been added on to the original polygonal shell keep. At the western end of the remaining walls two parallel slots for timber reinforcement in the thickness of the curtain can still be made out. An 18th century cannon still graces this part of the wall, standing sentinel over the River Honddu.

Speed's drawing of the castle illustrating his map of Brecknock shows the castle occupying the centre of an egg-shaped mound between the rivers Usk and Honddu. Access to the town was by a stone bridge of three arches, at the western end of which was the castle gatehouse attached to what appears to have been a polygonal shell keep. This keep is not shown standing on a motte, though in

94

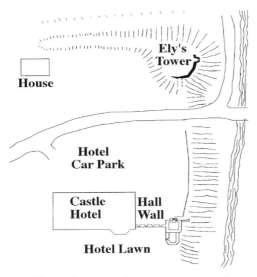

House

Ely's Tower

Hotel Car Park

Castle Hotel

Hall Wall

Hotel Lawn

Plan of the castle as it is presently

other respects Speed's drawing seems to tally quite well with current remains. The plan shows that the castle was divided into two wards. The northern ward contained the main buildings and the shell keep. A gateway leads to the southern chamfered triangular ward which encloses much of the area where the Castle Hotel gardens now lie. The ruins of this wall are still apparent in an 18th century print. Buck's illustration of the castle in 1732 shows the current hall wall, but without battlements, with a tower on its eastern end, Ely's Tower on the motte behind, and traces of a building to the west of the hall where the hotel now stands. It may be that part of the hotel immediately adjacent to the hall represents a solar range which could well have been the hall used by the Council of the Marches.

By 1808 the *Cambrian Traveller's Guide* referred to 'the magnificent castle ... which is now curtailed to a very insignificant ruin, and that little is so choked up and disfigured with miserable

Buck's illustration of the castle in 1732

95

habitations, as to exhibit no token of its ancient grandeur.' After 1809 the Morgans of Tredegar Park bought the castle and spent large amounts of money repairing the house attached to the present ruins and converting it into the Castle Hotel. An 1865 guide commented: 'Of the castle some scanty remains are now enclosed in the grounds attached to the principal inn, which on account is called the Castell Hotel.' A print in the Castle Hotel shows the present remains with the ruined curtain wall in front of them. This complements the evidence of the Buck print and the Speed plan for the line of the castle defences, well in front of the present remains.

The build of the 13th century hall wall is quite different from that of the remains of the shell keep. It stands apparently two stories high above present ground level and is topped by a fine post-medieval set of battlements which also crown the marginally higher towers to the east. This upper part of the structure almost certainly dates to the late 18th or early 19th century.

The base of the hall wall is slightly splayed and almost hidden within the splay are four narrow loops, illuminating what was the basement. Above these are four tall, narrow cusped windows, which have sockets in the jambs for iron frames. Behind these are deeply recessed arches with seats set in the approximately 2.6m thick wall. There is no trace of a northern wall, or any cross walls of a hall, though excavations have revealed bases for columns which would have supported the floor of the hall. There does not appear to have been any access between the eastern tower and the hall. Such is most unlikely in any true medieval structure, though a multitude of alterations and reinforcements to the wall may have obscured original openings.

An external and internal examination of the two 'mural towers' confirms a hotpotch of different construction dates. The two towers have been described collectively as a half round tower butted onto by a slightly later polygonal garderobe tower, but close inspection suggests other possibilities. The towers are entered through a fine 14th century shoulder-headed doorway, via an external stair against the west wall of the polygonal tower. The doorway, similar to those at Wigmore Castle, is non-medieval in positioning, though its pieces may well be genuine, and are possibly taken from another part of the castle ruins. Above and to the south of this doorway is the northern half of a fine arrow-slit. The southern half is irregular and obviously relaid; perhaps door and slit were rebuilt at the same time. In the opposite east wall are another arrow slit, which appears to have been added, and a simple loop. The quoins of the tower appear irregular and the whole is made up of a mass of rubble blocks of grey and old red sandstone, of which grey predominates. Much of the mortar in the lower part of the building has disintegrated.

The walls of the 'latrine' tower are only about 1.3m thick. This is thin for a defensive wall of a medieval castle tower but acceptable for a later insertion. Inside the structure is a small sub-rectangular room which has a relatively modern concrete floor. Beneath this is a basement apparently only entered by an external flue to the east. Presumably this is why the structure has been called a garderobe tower. As far as inspection of the now very unstable building could ascertain, there is no trace of any garderobes in this floor or apparently in those above. Neither are there any other flues. The state of the interior totally precluded reaching the third floor, but from what could be seen from lower levels no latrines could be postulated. From the first floor chamber, entrance was gained via three modern concrete steps, into what has been described as the half round tower.

Inside the 'round tower' is another sub-rectangular room. Internally there is virtually no trace of the slight exterior curve of this wall. Indeed its south wall seems entirely straight. A quarter round tower at a right-angled corner is to my knowledge unknown in any medieval structure, let alone a castle. The walls of this tower are again only about 1.3m thick, and once again windows and arrowslits juggle and encroach uncomfortably upon one another. Three arrowslits, one on each floor, indeed occupy the junction between the 'round' section of the tower and the rectangular structure to the north. The plinth, with its string course at its junction with the wall, does have an air of antiquity about it.

The western internal wall of the chamber within the 'round' tower has a chamfered corner built with fine quoins. However, at second floor level and higher these features become very irregular and there is a suspicion that they may be post-medieval. Beyond this 'tower', through another 14th century doorway in another insubstantial wall, is the current wooden staircase that allowed visitors excellent views from atop this 'viewing platform'. This once had concrete floors, though they are now largely collapsed. In the south-east corner of the stair chamber is a badly damaged, nearly 3m thick, rubble-built wall. This is almost certainly medieval and must be a part of the original castle, shrouded in the masonry of the later tower. Unfortunately, the wooden staircase, which so neatly fits into this chamber, is now in a state of collapse preventing safe access to the upper floors. It is clear that much of this rear section has been a late addition, and that some of the other work to the towers is later strengthening work.

Little now remains of Brecon's town defences. Bernard Neufmarché and his barons initially granted burgages within the castle defences, and as late as 1610 St Mary's Church was still regarded as the castle chapel! The 13th century walled town lay to the east of the Honddu, as shown in both Meredith Jones' and Speed's maps. According to Speed's plan the wall after leaving the castle bridge, at the top of High Street, was pierced by what appears to be the rectangular North or Struet Gate which allowed access to the road that ran through the suburbs to the priory. From here a curtain wall ran via several towers to the East Gate at the Watton Ward. The wall then continued down towards the Usk and then above it, along the course of Captain's Walk and via several more towers to the West Gate which commanded a bridge over the Usk to Llanfaes. Next to this was the Water Gate which allowed access to a bridge over the mouth of the Honddu. From the Water Gate the wall dog-legged (according to Speed) back to the castle gate. The wall towers seem to have been rectangular, though some were possibly round or D-shaped. Little now remains of these defences except to the east. Here, beyond the cattle market, is a 10m high bank, now much mutilated and pierced by modern roads. At its southern end there are the remains of what appears to have been a rectangular tower about 5m by 3m internally. Beyond this nothing of the town defences seem to have survived. The gates were apparently demolished in 1785 and probably the wall did not survive much longer.

Aberyscir

Motte with masonry remains
Location: 2.5 miles west of Brecon (SO 000 295)
Access: The castle lies beyond the gardens of a private house,
but can be glimsped from the A40 on the opposite side of the
River Usk

The wood between 'Abreschir' and Brecon, formerly the property
of Bernard fitz Unspac, was mentioned between 1191 and 1208.
This Bernard was a contemporary of William the Conqueror and a
prominent follower of the Mortimers as well as being the ancestor
of the Bramptons of Brampton Bryan. He died sometime in the reign

of Henry I. The wood then passed into the hands of the Waldeboefs, major honourial barons of Brecon lordship. As their neighbours were the Burghills and Poers of Fenni, the land south of the road between Brecon and Aberyscir, it seems possible that the castle of Aberyscir was the work of Bernard fitz Unspac and his Waldeboef successors. The castle itself seems never to have been mentioned in recorded history.

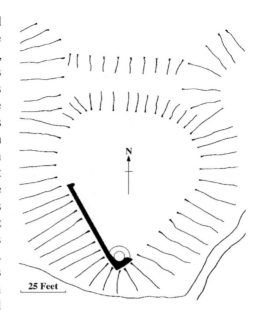

25 Feet

At Aberyscir, opposite the ruins of the old Roman fort, is a motte, 20m by 30m across its top, set on a spur projecting out into the River Usk. On the south and west side of this mound are the remains of a large shell keep or small inner ward. This consists of a robbed 2m wide wall running some 10m along the west side of the motte top. A slim, heavily damaged external batter can also be made out, set as it is on the edge of the mound. It has no berm. Externally the wall stands about 2m high, but internally it is about level with current ground level. At the south end of the motte are the foundations of a small round tower, about 8m in external diameter. This internal tower seems to sit upon a right-angled junction of the wall as evidenced by the right-angled batter beneath it. This suggests that this curved tower wall appears to be no more than a folly. The foundations of a southern wall set off from under this 'tower' to the east, where it fades out amongst the overgrown and uneven surface of the ovoid motte.

The remaining castle masonry seems to have been constructed of well chosen mortared rubble blocks, some of which have obviously been cut. The thin 'tower' wall may just be a robbed core of

100

a rectangular internal corner tower that has been re-mortared and shaped to appear as if it is a face. Certainly it does not match up to the foundations beneath it. This wall has recently been re-mortared by the house owners, as apparently it had also been 15 years ago. D.J. Cathcart King considered this structure to be a summer house, mainly due to its walls being only 0.2m thick. In fact the wall can be seen to have been robbed and the foundations suggest that they were originally over 2m thick. This strongly suggests a 12th century masonry castle which probably suffered a similar fate as the rest of the castles of the district in the 13th century.

Aberyscir ringwork

Possible castle ringwork
Location: A quarter of a mile north of Aberyscir Castle
(SO 001 298)
Access: On private land by the minor road

Only a quarter of a mile north of Aberyscir Castle is a distinct hummock of ground commanding the course of the Afon Ysgir as it cuts between the castle and the Roman fort on its way to the River Usk. It appears possible that this rise of ground was once crowned with a ringwork about 20m in diameter. This is now heavily denuded, but what appears to be a ditch is still evident on the vulnerable west of the site. If this is a castle it would seem to echo similar 'siege' ringworks at Castle Madog and Pont Estyll. As such it should probably be dated to the campaigns of Llywelyn Fawr between 1217 and 1234.

Alexanderstone

Motte and Bailey
Location: 1.5 miles north-east of Brecon (SO 073 301)
Access: Lies next to a footpath by the farm; can also be seen from the A470

Alexanderstone is only briefly mentioned in recorded history, but this suggests that it was built early as a fee of Brecon and was held by the Mora family, of whom one may have been called Alexander. An Alexander (no surname) witnessed a charter of David, Bishop of St David's concerning Brecon Priory around 1148. The mound is said to have been called 'Mara Mota', Walter Mara being the lord of Little Hereford in Herefordshire who held land of the lordship of Brecon towards the end of the 12th century.

After 1422, when the Bohun lands had been divided between the king and the Countess of Stafford, Alexanderstone was again mentioned because 12 marks a year had been taken from the profits of the manor and handed to John Brugge, esquire to the Commons, since 8 April 1417. From this record and the non-mention of the castle, it seems quite apparent that the now greatly antiquated fortress was derelict.

The castle consists of an irregular ditched motte 5m high, 10m across the motte top north to south and 15m east to west. To the north there is the site of a small horseshoe-shaped bailey, about 30m east to west by 15 north to south. It is now largely ploughed out, though traces of ditch and rampart can still be seen. The farm-house to the south may possibly be built on a further bailey.

Castle Madog

Motte
Location: 1 mile north of Lower Chapel, near the B4520
(SO 024 369)
Access: In grounds of private house, just visible from the B road

Castle Madog motte stands in the gardens of the impressive Castell Madog House, 6 miles north of Brecon. It has been heavily damaged over the centuries and its original dimensions can no longer be given with certainty. It is approximately 4m high and although still steep to the west, has a gentle slope to the east. The motte top is now an irregular ellipse about 3m across east to west and slightly less north to south. No trace of the bailey remains. There is also no known tenurial history for the site. As it is so close to Brecon it is to be assumed that its provenance is as the caput of an early Norman mesne fee. The tradition that the castle was held by the Powells since the first Norman conquest of the area, seems to be based on genealogical fabrication rather than attested historical fact. However, such tradition cannot be dismissed out of hand without detailed research into the family history.

Castle Madog Ringwork

Ringwork
Location: 1 mile north of Lower Chapel, near the B4520
(SO 025 370)
Access: In fields beside the B4520, clearly visible from the road

The small ringwork stands on a ridge-end site overlooking the Nant Fawr, a tributary of the River Honddu, in whose valley both castle sites stand. From this prominence the ringwork overlooks the motte some 75m to the south-west. The ringwork is roughly square with rounded corners and dominates the area, and even some of the high ground to the east. In this respect is siting is somewhat superior to that of Castle Madog motte.

In the late 1960s three small scale excavations were undertaken which disproved the idea that the earthworks marked the site of a Roman fortlet. The rampart was originally about 1.5m high and about 5m wide and made from small, loose stones set in soil containing marl. The collapse of this was suggested as one reason for the excavators finding no trace of any timberwork within the castle. Charcoal was discovered on the old ground surface beneath the rampart suggesting that the site was cleared by burning before construction commenced. The ditch was found to be 5m wide and a little under 1.5m deep, showing that the material for the rampart originated from the ditch, as could have been expected. There was no sign of a counterscarp bank.

A 4m by 5m area of the interior was excavated and no traces of any internal buildings were found, though several pottery shards and a prick spur of '12th century character' was uncovered. The third dig took place in the eastern 'entrance' to the ringwork. This showed that both flanks of the ringbank had a rough covering of stones to mark the 'gateway'. The entrance was also metalled with very small stones, with a 'kerb' of four large stones placed across half the width of the enclosure below the metalling.

Taken together, this evidence shows that the castle's occupation span was at best transitory. Its purpose would therefore seem to be either as a work camp for the construction of the motte, or a siege camp. The latter seems far more likely and although a time of around 1168 when the Lord Rhys was ravaging Brecknock might be possible, the dispute of 1230 seems a much more likely date.

To the north the little brook has been dammed by an earthwork to create a small lake north and west of the ringwork. This is on the castle's strongest side so it would seem unlikely that the water-works were specifically defensive, although they undoubtedly helped protect the site. The dam is said to be related to the stocking of rainbow trout in the last century.

Cilwhybert (or Modrydd)

> Motte
> Location: 2 miles south-west of Brecon (SO 014 268)
> Access: Can be easily seen from minor road in front of
> Cilwhybert Farm

The name of this site is probably originally Cilgilbert—'the valley of Gilbert'. Presumably then this castle was the stronghold of Gilbert, held as a mesne fee of Brecon lordship after 1093. Its history after this date is problematical, although the nearby ringwork is probably of Welsh provenance and suggests that the castle was besieged. A date for such a siege would seem best suited to one of the campaigns by Llywelyn Fawr in 1223, 1231 or 1233. It is quite possible that the castle fell sometime in this period and was never rebuilt.

The castle today consists of a tall, 5m high motte with a 14m diameter summit. This is set in a deep ditch with a 2m high counterscarp to the west. Presumably the bailey stood under the present farmhouse. Various amateur excavations are said to have found very large boulders in the mound's make up. Is this a possible indication of a tower upon the motte?

Clawdd British

Partial ringwork
Location: 5 miles north-north-west of Trecastle (SN 862 369)
Access: Lies on the Sennybridge Artillery Range!

Clawdd British, or as it now seems to have been re-christened, Clawdd Brythonig, above Llandeilo'r-fan, is a work similar in position and extent to Wuan Gunllwch (see below). It stands 340m above sea level on a fairly steep slope. On the uphill side is a 2m high 'ringbank' with a 1m deep ditch before it and a counterscarp. Like Wuan Gunllwch the ringwork defences are not carried through to the downhill side. Much of the material for the bank seems to have been dug from inside the ringwork and the ditch is fed from the numerous moorland brooks.

This castle may, like Wuan Gunllwch, date to the incursions of Llywelyn Fawr into the lordship of Brecon in the 1230s, but its positioning, away from any settlement and cultivation, is peculiar.

Cwm Camlais

Remains of a castle tower
Location: 2.5 miles south-east of Sennybridge (SN 956 261)
Access: Lies on farmland on moors

Cwm Camlais Castle stands on a prominent rise of ground nearly 370m above sea level. It has no known history other than the mid-14th century record that the land round about had been given to Einion Sais by Earl Humphrey Bohun (1221-1275, or 1265-98) to strengthen the castle of Camlais. This tells us nothing about the castle's provenance. It may have been built by Llywelyn ap Gruffydd in his period of dominance in Brycheiniog, in which case it might have been the castle destroyed by the Lord Edward in 1265. This in turn could explain Earl Humphrey Bohun wanting it strengthened in the late 1270s, having only reconquered this part of Brycheiniog from Llywelyn in 1276. The present state of the castle suggests that it is unlikely that Einion did anything to help preserve the fortress and it is never mentioned again. It would seem likely

107

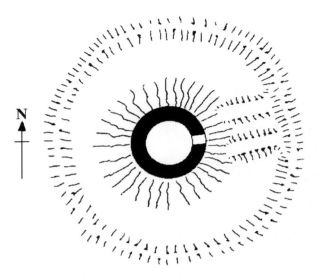

that this is the lost castle of Einion Sais of Penpont, as it stands only 1 mile from the traditional site on flat ground at SN 973 286.

The castle consists of the stump of a round tower still standing under its shroud of rubble and turf some 7m high. (The photograph shows excavations at the keep gate). The castle is about 14m in external diameter and has walls just over 3m thick. The interior of the tower still consists of a fine rubble ashlar to the south, and in the early 1980s a ground floor doorway was excavated to the east but has since been covered up. The tower is surrounded by a ditch and counterscarp, but has no bailey.

Hay-on-Wye Castle

> Major masonry ringwork, with surviving tower and gateway
> Location: In the centre of Hay-on-Wye (SO 229 424)
> Access: Open to Public from Castle Bookshop, and can be
> viewed from the market place to its south

Hay-on-Wye Castle was probably commenced early in the Norman invasion of Brycheiniog possibly simultaneously with Castell Dinas. Before 1155 the castle was far enough developed to have houses within it, for by this date one of them was granted to Brecon Priory by Earl Roger Hereford. The castle seems to have been a favoured residence of Matilda St Valery, the wife of William Braose who was also recorded as Maud de la Hay. Hay Castle was seized by King John in 1208 and garrisoned on his behalf until retaken by the Braose brothers in 1215. In August 1216 it was apparently abandoned to King John, who burnt both town and castle. Rebuilt by Reginald Braose, Hay Castle was attacked by Llywelyn Fawr in 1231 when the town was burned. Soon after 22 July, Walter Godarville, the constable of the castle, was tricked by the monks of

Cwmhir and led into an ambush in the River Wye nearby; perhaps the town was burned after this disaster rather than before as the chronicles seem to suggest. In 1233 Hay Castle became Henry III's base for his operations against Walter Clifford of Cantref Selyf, and was strengthened after many of the castles of Brecknock had been stormed by the rebels and Prince Llywelyn.

In March 1263 the castle was seized from Humphrey Bohun Junior, to whom it had passed, and given to Roger Mortimer. In July 1264 the Castle, under Mortimer's constable, Walter Hackelutel, surrendered to the army of Earl Simon Montfort of Leicester and his confederate barons. Roger Mortimer, supporting the future Edward I, retook the castle during the campaigns of 1265 and used it as a base for his unsuccessful attack on Brecon Castle in May 1266. The castle was then passed to Earl Gilbert Clare who returned it to the Bohuns. They in turn successfully used it as a base to attack Brecon Castle in 1273. The castle, like so many others in the Middle March, was seized by the Crown in the warfare of 1322.

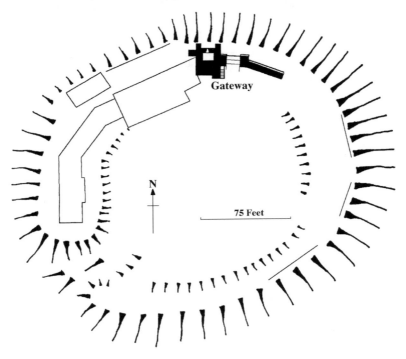

Gateway

N

75 Feet

The value of Hay Castle with its appurtenances was £50 in 1362, rising to £51 in 1372, which suggests that it outlived many of the mesne castles of the county. In 1372 the porter of the castle still received 8d per week wages, with an allowance of 6s 8d for his yearly expenses. The following year Richard Mogholom was bailiff of Hay Castle and claimed expenses for new locks on the castle gate and the lord's chamber. He also claimed for an iron chain and lock which was used to secure the lord's boat on the River Wye. Presumably this was a ferry, for similar vessels existed at both Builth Wells and Bredwardine.

The castle was garrisoned against Glyndwr and may have been sacked soon after the battle of Pilleth in 1402. It was subsequently repaired although it was again ruinous by 1461. When Leland entered Hay he found it standing close to the Wye and protected by a strong town wall which had 3 gates and a postern, whilst the castle was obviously in some decay, though 'sumtime hath bene right stately.'

The remains of Hay Castle dominate the town and surrounding district from its commanding position on the high ground some quarter of a mile south of the Wye. A fraction over a mile away to the north-west lies a similar 'ringwork' set on a knoll at Clyro, now in Radnorshire. Three quarters of a mile to the south-east of Hay Castle, at Cusop, (SO 240 415) stands another 'ringwork'. All three had masonry defences consisting of a stone polygonal enclosure and taken as a unit, like the Trilateral of Skenfrith, Grosmont and White Castle to the south, effectively block a lowland routeway out of Wales. A similar foundation date for all three castles may therefore be postulated.

The 'ringwork' under the masonry remains at Hay is about 70m by 80m across and has a roughly east-west orientation. The castle occupies the entire summit of the small knoll and it seems likely that the earthwork defences are entirely natural, although scarped to produce a steeper approach to south, east and west. The entrance to the south-west, where the western 'bank' has been removed, is almost certainly modern to allow vehicular access to the house. The gateway to the south also shows that the interior of the enclosure is filled with some 2m of debris, as appears common with most masonry castles.

The earliest masonry structure is undoubtedly the four-storied rectangular tower which, in spite of the later mansion attached to it, still dominates the town. The tower has been heavily rebuilt over the years, partly due to having very poor foundations. At an early date buttresses had to be added to the tower, at three, if not all four corners; a buttress at the fourth corner may have been destroyed by the building of the mansion. Even with this strengthening, the north-west corner is still sagging and cracking dramatically. It is hard to judge what form this tower took originally due to these multiple rebuildings. The south-east corner has been totally replaced at some point from the foundations to the roof, and the internal corner chamfered off internally for greater strength. It would appear that this rebuilding included the insertion of the current doorway, possibly in the position of the original entrance. The external stairway probably also dates from this rebuilding, perhaps replacing an earlier wooden one. The south-west corner appears to have been totally rebuilt when the mansion was built abutting onto the tower in the 17th century. The two northern corners were heavily buttressed at least during the first part of the 18th century, and probably substantially earlier, to help support the crumbling tower foundations. The entire north wall of the tower and possibly also the southern wall have been totally rebuilt from the foundations upwards. It seems likely that they had older (original?) windows reset in them during this rebuilding. The east and west walls have also been heavily rebuilt, but not as completely as their associates. In spite of this rebuilding there is no evidence that this tower was originally complemented by other stone defences, all the remaining walls forming butt joints. It therefore seems likely that this tower was originally built as a free-standing structure on top of the current castle knoll. Most likely a wooden palisade crowned the rest of the rise. It is almost certain that any entrance to the site was on the town or north side as today. Therefore the tower would seem to have been built to protect any such entrance. As both its north and south walls have been totally rebuilt it is not impossible that this structure started life as an early, Exeter style, square gatehouse, which was later converted to a (residential?) tower when the stone gateway was added to its east side. Alternatively it may have covered an earlier entrance in the position of the current one.

The tower today still stands 3½ stories high, and, judging from Buck's print of 1741, this is only some ten feet lower than its original battlemented height. The ground floor is currently three-quarters filled with rubble in an attempt to provide some extra stability to the foundations, as well as providing a first floor viewing platform for the interior of the tower. The only window visible on the ground level, (there may be another buried one to the south), is a cross between a splayed window and a window set in a narrow embrasure. Its style is Norman, but it is undoubtedly reset, possibly originally having come from higher up the same wall. The stacked rubble precludes any examination of the interior of the other three walls. What can be seen externally, however, in the east and west walls, are the eroded remnants of a string course set at the junction between the ground and first floors. Traces of a further string course between the first and second floors were still visible in Buck's day, although this part of the wall has now collapsed. This higher string course is set in the south wall, but this is almost certainly re-laid.

The first floor of the tower is undoubtedly the most interesting. Entrance is gained by the Early English pointed doorway in the east wall, where the walls are some 1.8m thick. This door, with a very shallow draw-bar slot, gives the only medieval external access to the tower. The room entered by this doorway consists of a single chamber with two late medieval twin lights set in the north wall, with a fireplace in between, and a single twin light window to the south, just like the second floor above it. To the west, on the first floor, is a blocked late doorway connecting to the mansion. The second floor is similar to the first, except the only access is by the blocked doorway to the adjoining mansion on the west side and to the apparent remains of a small chamber in the north-east corner. The round-headed twin light window to the south is a fine early example, even if the central limestone mullion is missing. It may be in its original position, even if the wall beneath it has been rebuilt and the window below reset. Between these two southerly-facing windows are much later dove roosts, built into the external wall of the tower. The top floor of the tower is now mostly destroyed. Buck's print shows that there were two flat headed windows to the north and suggests a parapet with one merlon remaining to the south-east. The blocked lower half of another 17th century doorway can still be traced in the east wall, even though, when considering Buck's print, this would appear to be above the mansion roof level. The tower walls themselves are made of local shale set in a random coursed range, rubble style. None of the corner quoins appear original, but it would appear that the window quoins are limestone, and as such may have been 'imported'. This in turn may show some affluence in the builders.

But when was this tower built and for what purpose? The walls are only 1.8m thick and this would suggest an early date. Such thin walls preclude wall stairs and with the apparent lack of external doors it must be assumed that access to the higher levels was attained by internal wooden stairs, or possibly even ladders. Buck's view shows a considerable plinth to the north, though this is now buried. Such a plinth, if original, would likely preclude the structure from having originally been a gatehouse. Therefore it seems best to accept this tower as having been built as early lodgings or a very early square keep—a very plain pre-cursor of that found at Goodrich Castle. Such a tall, narrow tower may perhaps be best thought of as a watchtower commanding the plain of the Wye and visible from its companion tower at Clyro and possible also Cusop. If this suggested scenario is correct, it would point to a time when Hay and Clyro were under the same lordship. By 1095, if not earlier, Elfael (now southern Radnorshire) was held by the Tosny family and Hay-on-Wye was a part of Brecon lordship. It seems, therefore, that a common origin would have to precede that date. The most obvious time would thus have been in the period 1067 to 1075 when the earls of Hereford were penetrating Brycheiniog down the Wye valley and a distinction between the lordships of Elfael and Brecon had not yet been drawn. Indeed, disputes continued into the late 13th century between the two lords and their vassals concerning the ownership of various lands on the north bank of the Wye. Consequently it would appear likely that the Wye valley, 'my tenements along the Wye', were held by the earls of Hereford. Such an early date for this 'weak' tower is neither impossible nor unlikely, though currently unprovable and would again emphasise the early Norman conquest of Brycheiniog. This suggestion for an early foundation for all three sites is strengthened by the tenurial history of Cusop. At Domesday Cusop (Cheweshope) was recorded as one parcel of land that belonged to Kingstone, a property previously held by William fitz Osbern as Earl of Hereford, and currently held by Roger Lacy, a prominent warrior who held various lands from the gift of the earls of Hereford. These three castles may therefore have been built in the period prior to 1070, when Earl William was securing his Saxon lands prior to dealing with the Welsh problem. This would have given him both a frontier against Welsh aggression, which is well attested along this route at this time, and a secure base from which to launch his conquest of Brycheiniog and Gwent.

The next phase in the castle's development would seem to be the replacement of the suggested palisade around the knoll with a polygonal stone wall. Most of this wall has now vanished, but that to the east of the tower still stands to nearly full height and to the east and south the foundations can still be easily traced. One of the most interesting points about this perimeter wall is that it appears, once again, to have no flanking structure like many other similar enclosure castles, with only one square tower, *viz* Clyro and Cusop, and Lydney and St Briavels in Gloucestershire. Once again this may suggest an early pre-1075 date for the masonry of the curtain, although it must here be stressed that such castles appear common throughout at least the 12th century. The most important remnant of this curtain is undoubtedly the finely built gateway, now encased by the later gatehouse. This encasing has undoubtedly given the gateway greater protection from the elements than is seen at other sites, allowing the survival of what is undoubtedly a splendidly carved ashlar entrance. The gateway projects slightly from the wall in a manner that almost, but not quite, provides flanking. This again suggests an early date. The archway is sharply pointed and has a string course at the top of the jambs that stretches along under the encasing gatehouse wall, but does not align with the string course of the tower.

Encasing the earlier Norman gateway is a later gatehouse which, unlike the gate it protects, is a 'jerry-built' structure. Its most striking feature is its arches which encase the earlier Norman gate to north and south, for they are dramatically unbalanced. This asymmetry is not the result of collapse, but of poor planning. Much of this work is barely attached to the older gate and suggests that this was thrown up in a hurry to protect a vulnerable entrance. Many attacks and rebuildings of the castle are either attested or implied by the castle's history in the period 1216 to 1266 and it would seem likely that the building dates to this period. Inside the entrance, another stairway has been added to reach the portcullis room over the gate. From here the portcullis that dropped in front of the Norman gate could be operated, the main purpose for this addition to the castle defences. This room is an oblong chamber which appears to have never been roofed, but was battlemented to the north, and probably likewise on two other sides, although these have since disappeared. The fourth side abutted the tower. The battlements to the north are little more than show defences, being about 0.5m thick, although a cross arrow slit does pierce the central merlon. Such details are generally dated to the mid-13th century and there seems no reason to doubt this. Below this room on the main tower's east wall, one springer of an arch projects awkwardly from the doorway. This would undoubtedly have formed another door similar to the one to the tower, and would have given access to the stairway up to the portcullis room.

It would seem likely that access to the curtain wall-walk would have been gained from the gatehouse portcullis room. No other evidence for access to the higher levels of the castle exists, although there must have been earlier stairs. An internal building may have lain alongside the curtain to the east of the entrance although only excavation could prove this now. At the top of this well-preserved piece of wall is a corbelled out projection running the entire length of the internal curtain. If this were not a roofing level of an internal building it would probably be best interpreted as the lowest courses of a stone parapet. As such it suggests that this curtain is standing to its full height bar the battlements. Externally the wall has an impressive battered plinth which is now almost totally devoid of mortar. A similar narrower plinth exists internally. Both appear to be later shoring operations and both may be post-medieval. Certainly, Buck's print shows the curtain as plain here, but the plinth, if existing then, would appear to be buried under a garden and small retaining wall, set on the scarp. All the later buttressing of the gatehouse and tower can also be seen in place, as is a cobbled ramp that runs up to the gatehouse, and terracing in front of the mansion. As a final point it should be noted that the door in place in the print has remarkable similarities to the one still in position. Is this one of our few remaining medieval castle doors?

Hay-on-Wye Motte

Motte
Location: Near St Mary's Church, in the west of Hay-on-Wye
(SO 226 422)
Access: On private land, but visible from the road to the church

This small 3m high motte was probably built by William Revel in the last years of the 12th century in his fee of Hay-on-Wye. The castle would appear to have remained separate from Hay-on-Wye Castle which remained in the hands of the lord of Brecon. The manor of Melinog, a part of Hay fee mentioned in about 1115 when the church of St Mary was dedicated, remained independent of the main Hay Castle throughout the medieval period and the same may have been true of this motte by the church. The castle was certainly abandoned and in its current condition by the 1540s when Leland visited the site, describing it as 'a great rounde hille of yerth cast up by mennes hondes other for a wyndmille to stand upon or rather for sum fortress of bataille.'

The motte itself stands on a ledge above a small brook which has cut a deep gorge into the surrounding sub-soil as it empties into the nearby River Wye. On the other, western, bank of this stream is the heavily rebuilt parish church, of which only the lower courses of the tower show much evidence of having been a Norman foundation. The motte itself is about 13m in diameter. On the north side of the mound a recent tree fall (before 1984) revealed the gravelly make up of the interior together with some loose rubble. Leading to the north towards the Wye and east towards the town, is a platform which may have supported a bailey. This has recently been levelled for the town market and any such defences have been obliterated.

Llanddew (Bishop's Castle)

Assorted masonry and other remains
Location: In the centre of Llanddew, north-east of Brecon
(SO 054 308)
Access: The most extensive masonry remains lie in the
grounds of a guest house, but can be partially viewed
from the roads, as can the rest of the remains

It is often stated that a 14th century Bishop's Palace was built at Llanddew. The idea that this palace was built by Bishop Gower seems totally erroneous, apparently relying on a statute made by him in 1342 when he decreed that only six places of residence together with Llanddew were to be supported and maintained. The statute in fact implies that the palace was already in existence and was not built by him. Indeed, the ruins appear to be of a much older structure, though Bishop Gower's well is probably of his provenance.

In Leland's day the palace had become 'wher was sumtime a very faiyre place of the bisshops, now no thing but an onsemeli ruine. The arch-diacon of Breeknock hath a house even there, and that is also fallen downe for the more part.' These remains are what is left of Llanddew Castle overlooking the cruciform church in the centre of the village.

The ruins consist of one relatively well preserved stretch of curtain wall along the west side of the castle perimeter. Little if any mortar remains in this structure and the wall is in a state of almost terminal collapse. The small, half-round, solid drum tower which has been added half-way down the curtain is likewise in imminent danger of collapse. No architectural features or details remain in this masonry, though just south of the drum tower is the stagnant pool of Bishop Gower's well. Next to it is an early 20th century pump. On the interior side of the wall is an over-grown and half buried flight of steps down to the main well which would have supported the

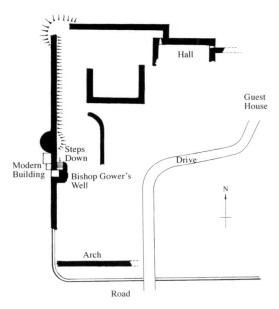

119

garrison. The well is said to have been constructed by Bishop Gower in the 14th century and has little to recommend it as a defensive structure. At the south end of the curtain the wall simply fades out, and above this is a pleasant little paved area entered from the house garden by a fine medieval doorway which appears to be set in a modern wall. The road frontage bounds what was probably the old line of the castle precinct to the south. At the eastern extreme of the castle a low bank runs off to the north. This is almost certainly the site of a curtain wall similar to that which still stands to the west. After about 30m the 'wall' makes a right-angled turn to the west for about 15m and then turns again to the north.

After a short distance the main remaining feature of the castle is reached, the hall. This building, quite likely the 'small residence' of Giraldus Cambrensis, is about 22m long by 8m wide internally. Little now remains of it except for the east wall and the north-west corner. Both these fragments stand at least two stories high. The east fragment, heavily overgrown, shows evidence of a large main window at first floor level. This window was in the external wall. The other fragment has a small, heavily robbed, first floor window which, like its apparently much larger counterpart to the east, was also external. In the basement of the hall, in the west wall, is a small window set in a deep splay which might easily be 12th century in construction. From the north-west corner of the hall the curtain wall made its irregular way back via two right-angled turns to the solid drum tower on the western wall of the enceinte. One right-angled corner still stands some 2 metres high, while elsewhere the now entirely un-mortared curtain stands some 20 courses high.

Giraldus, on being told of William Braose's seizure of the temporalities of St David's probably in 1202 wrote that he cheered his companions on whilst returning from Ceredigion with words which seem to allude to his palace at Llanddew: 'Have we not some good ale at home? Let us go and drink it before it be all gone.' The hall may also have been the venue for the trial of the earls of Hereford and Gloucester in 1291. The minimal architectural evidence might suggest that the hall was early 12th century and the irregular curtain adjoining it probably early 13th. The fortification of the ecclesiastical residence after the fall of Llywelyn ap Gruffydd in 1282 seems unlikely.

120

Llandefaelog-Fach

Motte
Location: 2 miles north of Brecon on the B4520 (SO 033 323)
Access: In the grounds of a private house, but can be glimpsed
from the footpath which runs along the stream to the
north of the site

This castle consists of a large motte on the opposite side of the road to the church. It is now heavily overgrown, but it seems to have been about 5m high with a motte top about 17m across. To the south of the mound on a platform where the bailey may have been, is a fine house with an armorial slab of 1630. In the church is a fine carved pillar with an effigy of a local Dark Age dignitary, Brochmail, cut on it. Llandefaelog-Fach was possibly the castle of the Poitevins (deriving from Poitou) who are said to have owned a castle in this district, although the traditional site is behind Pytinglas farm at SO 034 317.

Llanigon or **Llanthomas**

> Motte
> Location: In Llanigon, south-west of Hay-on-Wye (SO 209 403)
> Access: Lies in the garden of a bungalow, but is plainly visible
> from the adjacent minor road

Llanigon Castle may have lain in the manor of Melinog or the Welshry of Hay-on-Wye. It has no known early history, but by 1521 the lordship of Llanthomas was held by the Lord Ferrers for half a knight's fee. It is therefore possible that this state of affairs dated back to the 1160s when Sibyl Braose had married Earl Ferrers of Tutbury! This lordship was possibly a small remnant of that once held by William Revel as the lordship of Hay. Welsh Hay appears to have lain in the high ground to the west and north of the town itself where Llanthomas is now.

The castle remains consist of a mutilated motte about 3m high and 10m diameter at its base, together with a slight surrounding rampart to the west. The site overlooks the steep-sided dingle of the Digedi Brook to the north. A bungalow was built in the 1980s on the platform to the north and west of the motte, but no trace of any enclosure was discovered during the construction. Instead, three stone filled 'features' were uncovered and a stone-filled 'pit or ditch butt-end' about 2 metres across. A slight bank to the south of the motte may indicate that the bailey lay under the present road.

Pencelli Castle

Foundations of major stone castle
Location: In Pencelli, alongside B4558 (SO 095 248)
Access: The keep and earthworks lie in the garden of Pencelli
House, but the site can be viewed from both the road
and the footpath by the canal

Pencelli Castle was probably built in the late 11th century by Ralph
Baskerville and quite likely saw service in the war of 1093 to 1099.
Robert, the last Baskerville lord of Pencelli, seems to have died
around 1210, perhaps as a victim of William Braose's war that
occurred in central Wales that summer. His lands then passed
through a daughter to the Le Wafre family, but were seized by
Reginald Braose in 1215. The Le Wafres regained seisin, but lost
the fortress and mesne lordship to rebel and Welsh forces in 1233.
The castle was subsequently rebuilt, but probably taken again in
1262. It was recovered by 1273, after which the twin towered gatehouse might have been built by Roger Mortimer Junior who had
acquired the castle probably through his father's agency. The
fortress was seized from Morimer by King Edward II in 1322 and
probably fell into decay soon afterwards.

The castle site, behind the Tudor house, consists of a triangular shelf of land thrusting into the flood plain of the River Usk. Towards the apex of this projection lies a mass of turfed over rubble in what could once, before its recent unpublished excavation, easily be mistaken as a motte. In fact it proved to be the ruin of a castle keep (see photograph at start of entry), buried in its own debris. Buck's print shows a single spike of masonry towering over the rest of the enceinte and a small excavation has revealed the 14m square foundations of a tall rectangular tower with walls about 3m thick. This has a stepped plinth base which is indicative of an early construction date. On the river side (east) is a 10m long structure abutting the tower face and which ends 3-4m short of the tower corner, in what appears to have been a projecting rectangular buttress. This seems quite clearly to be a later forebuilding to the tower entrance. To the north of the tower is a confused mass of fallen rubble from the tower, lying on what appears to be masonry foundations unearthed by the excavations. This may have been the site of service buildings. Here a single fragment of a stone roof tile was noticed.

Cutting off the spur of land, in which Pencelli House still stands, was a slight ditch enclosing an area of land about 33m by 25m. This was originally protected by a curtain wall with windows in it indicating that were structures backing onto it. In the centre was a fine twin towered gatehouse of which nothing now remains. About 120 metres beyond this line of defence is the remnant of another ward, which has been largely obliterated by the road. To the east and north the rampart and ditch, part of it in use as a duckpond, remains. In the house standing in the bailey of Pencelli Castle are one or two re-used features from the castle, particularly a loop and part of another in the east wall. Internally, the owner has discovered some medieval arches which may have formed part of the castle chapel. Judging from the state of the site when Buck visited, it can be assumed that much of the keep material ended up incorporated in the house, whilst stone from the gatehouse and curtain was possibly used for building much of the present outbuildings.

Pont Estyll

Ringwork
Location: 2 miles south-west of Brecon (SO 009 270)
Access: A public footpath runs from the bridge on the minor road
through the site

This is a small sub rectangular 'armchair'-shaped ringwork, directly overlooking the Afon Tarell to the south. It is possible that the southern part of the ring has been swept down the bank of the river, the rest being perched precariously on the terrace. In position and plan it is similar to the ringwork at Castle Madog, it too utilising running water as a defence and commanding a nearby motte castle. Pont Estyll ringwork is about 27m north to south and 35m east to west. The site has been much ploughed out and the ditch to the west is but a fragment of its former self. The rampart, much denuded, is less than 1m high. There is the possibility of a bailey on the northern, slightly higher, side, but this is by no means certain. There is no apparent entrance to the site, although if there was a bailey the castle gateway was no doubt to the north.

The castle may be a Welsh work of one of the campaigns of Llywelyn Fawr between 1217 and 1234, quite possibly being used as a siege castle for nearby Cilwhybert Castle.

Sennybridge

Remains of stone enclosure castle
Location: Towards western edge of Sennybridge (SN 920 284)
Access: Lies on private ground but can be glimpsed from a
lane to new houses off to the south of the A40

Possibly commenced soon after 1262 as Llywelyn's 'new castle above Brecon', it was certainly in the hands of Einion Sais (Einion the English speaker) by 1271 when he was found dating letters from Rhyd y Briw, near which the castle stands. Its plan is distinctly Welsh, and despite its lowland position it stands a fair chance of having been the major castle of Llywelyn in Brycheiniog.

The castle now consists of the remains of a D-shaped tower about 8m in external diameter with walls nearly 2m thick. This still stands at the end of a platform above a stream to a height of about 6m. North of this, running east to west across the site and connected by the remains of one wall to the tower, is what appears to have been a curtain wall and which makes a right-angled turn to the south at its eastern extreme. Beyond this turn, to the east, is a slight

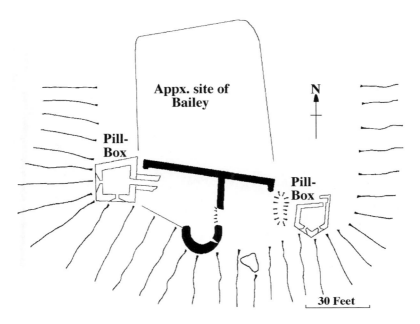

ditch before the remains of a concrete Second World War pill box which may occupy the site of a tower. At the western end of the site is another pill box, this time brick-built and with a slight forebuilding. Again it may overlie the site of another tower. The northern front of the castle is occupied by a modern bungalow and its garden. In plan this castle, with its possible towers at either extreme and a D-shaped tower in between, parallels the Welsh designs at Ewloe and Dolforwyn.

Trecastle

Motte and Bailey
Location: On eastern edge of Trecastle, north of the A40
(SN 882 291)
Access: The castle lies on private land, but can be
clearly seen from the A40

This castle, 260m above sea level, commands the upper reaches of the River Usk and the road that winds through the valley from Brecon to Llandovery. It is often thought of as a staging post on the westward route of Norman conquest, but it seems more likely that Llandovery was conquered by Richard fitz Pons, operating not from Brecon but from Carmarthen and Devon where he had a strong power base. The early history of Trecastle has been described as being 'involved in impenetrable darkness', as was noted over 100 years ago. Still holding true, an attempt will be made to shed some light on the history of this castle and its fate.

Trecastle probably means 'village of the castle' and so we may assume that the castle was founded at a virgin site for purely military reasons, and that the village grew up around it. As the castle or village does not have a personal name attached to it, it seems reasonable to suppose that it was built by the lord of Brecon, presumably by Bernard Neufmarché himself.

In 1121 it was stated by King Henry I that the land of Brecon bordered that of Llandovery, which may imply stable Norman control in this district and therefore a castle. If a castle had been built, it had probably been destroyed by 1136 when Baldwin Clare could only advance as far westwards as Brecon on his journey towards Cardigan. Presumably Trecastle, and Llandovery Castle beyond, had already fallen to the Welsh insurgents. In later eras the district around Trecastle was still held directly of the lord of Brecon, but this does not necessarily imply a continuity of tenure. What can be suggested is that any castle here did not survive the reign of Stephen and its possible successor was Sennybridge Castle, built by the Welsh lord of Defynnog. Against this, Trecastle may have been re-built in the late 1150s when Walter Clifford was campaigning again in the Llandovery region.

The castle was built on a vaguely defensible undulating ridge-end site, the motte being built on the uphill part of the ridge, defending the lower bailey at the apex of the site. The motte is about 8m high and aligned on a north-east to south-west axis, being 17m wide and 28m long. The mound has much loose rubble along the motte sides and it is possible that there was an elongated shell keep or tower here. There is a now badly silted ditch between the motte and bailey. South and west of the motte is the large 70m long bailey which seems to have been defended by a rampart, made of clayey soil and small slabs of old red sandstone, and ditch, though much of this has now been damaged. The entire site was apparently surrounded by a counterscarp bank, but this is now heavily denuded or destroyed.

Ty'n-y-Caeau

Mound
Location: 1.5 miles east of Brecon (SO 070 295)
Access: Is visible from the minor road to its west
(notably after leaf fall!)

This low, 1m high, 'motte' stands just above the little Slwch brook in a boggy field once criss-crossed by brooks. The motte measures only 9m in diameter at the top and is surrounded by a mostly filled ditch and slight counterscarp bank. There is no trace of a bailey, but there is a stream bed immediately to the north. Before modern drainage patterns were established this site must have been set in a marsh, and has construction of a very questionable nature. Was it a siege castle of Humphrey Bohun in the early 1270s or a fortified post set up by one of the Llywelyns as they attempted to take or hold Brecon? We may never know the answer, but its design does more probably suggest a Welsh origin.

Vaynor Castle

Motte and bailey
Location: 2 miles north of Merthyr Tydfil (SO 047 102)
Access: Visible from footpath leading south-west
from the ruined church

Vaynor Castle commands the valley of the Little Taff and marks the current boundary between the shires of Glamorgan and Brecon. In the 1290s this boundary seems to have been rather more problematical and this is what led to the brief Marcher war between the earls of Gloucester and Hereford. Quite likely the church of Vaynor was destroyed in this fighting, and possibly the castle also. The castle almost certainly predated that of Morlais opposite. (The photograph shows Morlais outlined on the ridge on the far side of the valley.)

The fortress consists of a 3m high motte set in a slight ditch on the very edge of the 30m deep gorge that descends to the Little Taff. No trace of any baileys now remain, probably due to agricultural activity on the site, but they could have existed to north, east and west. Alternatively there are several other Brecknock castles that consist solely of towers, and a lone motte may not be all that unlikely. As the top of the motte is cupped it may also be possible that the mound is merely the shroud of yet another destroyed round tower.

Ystradfellte or **Castell Coch**

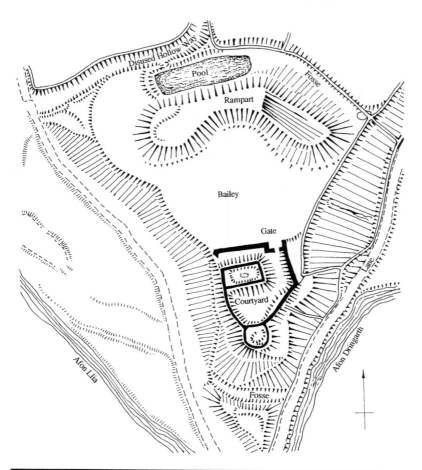

Earthworks and foundations
Location: 1 mile north-east of the centre of Ystradfellte
(SN 936 145)
Access: On private land, but much can be seen from the minor
road to its south and the public footpath to its east

Castell Coch was probably built in the early 13th century. Taken
over by the king in 1230 on the hanging of William Braose, it may
have been destroyed or occupied by Llywelyn before 1234. The

castle is suggested as a rather unlikely meeting point for Marcher forces in the war of 1276-77. In 1316 it served its last recorded purpose when Llywelyn Bren surrendered to the lord of Brecon here. Probably it did not long survive this era.

The castle is built in the upper reaches of the Afon Mellte in what has been described as 'an oasis, remote and difficult of access.' It is set on a triangular spur of land, some 10m north of the junction of two streams. On its northern 'open' front a massive rampart and ditch protects the site and cuts it off from the open ground. At the southern point of the triangle is a small triangular hornwork projecting out to the junction of the streams. Above this lies the main masonry heart of the castle. The focal point of the remains is the utterly ruined rectangular hall block, about 18m by 12m externally. This is orientated roughly east to west and has walls approximately 2m thick, except to the west where it forms part of the perimeter of the ward and appears to be twice as thick. This double thickness wall appears to indicate that the curtain was built against the hall, or vice versa. Whatever the case, it suggests that there are at least two masonry phases to the castle. North of the hall are slight remains of a curtain wall that defended the apex of the castle site. This is now but a poor shadow of its former self, indicated by a mound 0.6m high by about 1m wide. At the east end of this wall is an inset gateway about 1.5m wide. There appears to be no ditch defending either wall or gateway.

From the gateway the curtain wall ran southwards for some 20m before making an obtuse angle and continuing another 25m to a round tower at the southern apex of the site. The wall appears to be a little less than 2m thick and runs in two straight sections, broken by an obtuse junction. The round tower commands the southern apex of the castle site and probably stood at least 3 stories high. Currently it seems to have an internal diameter of 6m and walls 2.5m thick. There is an apparent ground floor access to the north.

The design of this castle seems specifically Welsh and of two periods, yet the castle is only ever mentioned in Norman hands. The design of a free standing rectangular tower or hall and a free standing round tower does seem to be exceptionally Welsh and is echoed in the Welsh castles of Machen, Ewloe, Dolbadarn, Dolforwyn and possibly Dinas Bran. All of these castles in North

Wales seem to have been envisaged by Llywelyn Fawr or his sons under his tutelage. Machen was probably built by Morgan ap Hywel of Caerleon with the aid of Llywelyn. It may, therefore, be that Ystradfellte Castle was the work of Llywelyn Fawr in the period 1215 to 1217 when he was working in harmony with Reginald Braose. In addition, the curtain wall and gatehouse may be the work of his grandson, Llywelyn ap Gruffydd, when he held the lordship of Brecon between 1262 and 1276 as the work seems far too irregular for Norman builders. Alternatively, the curtain may have been constructed by Llywelyn Fawr in the period 1234 to 1240 when he was putting pressure on the Marches of Wales.

Bronllys Castle

Masonry tower with motte and bailey
Location: Half a mile south-east of Bronllys on A479
(SO 149 346)
Access: Tower in care of CADW and open at all reasonable
times; bailey and forebuilding in private grounds

The castle was probably not founded until 1144 when Cantref Selyf was granted to Walter Clifford, the mesne tenant of the Tosnys at Clifford Castle. The grant was made for the service of 5 knights at Earl Miles of Hereford's castle of Brecon, though the castle itself was not mentioned. In the latter part of 1165 Miles Hereford was killed here whilst being entertained by Walter Clifford; in the middle of the night a fire gripped the castle and a stone fell from the principal tower onto his head. It is noticeable that the much altered round tower on the motte still shows signs of fire damage! After that fiasco, Bronllys Castle seems to have led a fairly quiet life, being the administrative centre of the Clifford's mesne lordship of Cantref Selyf, although the castle was seized by the Crown in 1233 during the Clifford Rebellion. Cantref Selyf was attacked by Prince Dafydd in 1241 and 1244, but no mention is made of the castle which undoubtedly held out. Like so many other fortresses it was seized by Edward II in 1322 after the Marcher rebellion of 1321. In 1349 the mesne lordship was annexed by Humphrey Bohun of Brecon and then it descended to his heirs, the earls of Lancaster. Consequently, Bronllys Castle became royal property on the accession of Henry IV, Earl of Lancaster, in 1399. The castle was probably still habitable in 1444 when Nicholas Poyntz, esquire, lord of Tretower in right of his Bluet wife, was granted the stewardship of the castle by the Crown together with the lordships of Pencelli and Cantref Selyf and the manors of Llangoed and Alexanderstone. These offices were later passed on to Sir Roger Vaughan in 1460. In 1521 the castle was said to be beyond repair and of use only as a prison. So many castles met a similar fate through neglect.

The castle consists of a large, tall round tower set on a natural outcrop of rock which has then been turfed over to look like an artificial motte. The tower has a vaulted basement with only one loop for light. The walls are about 3m thick and boast a fine plinth and string course. Internally are traces of timber reinforcements set within the walls. The ceiling of the basement is a medieval barrel vault, with concrete reinforcing above. This replaces an earlier lower ceiling. Was the first a wooden ceiling destroyed in the fire of 1165?

The first floor entrance is about 4m above the current motte-top and was previously reached by a forebuilding, the slight remnants of

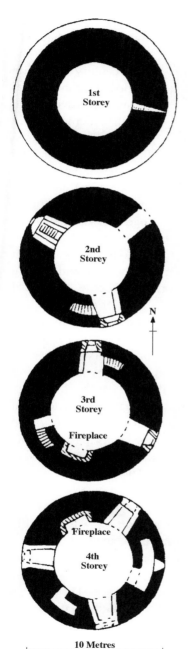

1st Storey

2nd Storey

N

3rd Storey

Fireplace

Fireplace

4th Storey

10 Metres

which are now enshrouded in vegetation in the garden below. Buck's print shows that this had been destroyed by 1741. The entrance door was bolted by a single drawbar, the holes for which still remain. The walls in the first floor are pierced by two deeply splayed recesses which house windows and access stairs to the upper and lower floors. As in the basement it can be seen that the ceiling of this room has been raised, the earlier corbels being replaced by slightly higher beam holes. The curving mural stair leads up to the second floor, which like its predecessor boasts two windows. There is also a raised ceiling level. This room has a large fireplace that probably replaces an earlier model. Notice the lamp brackets on each side of the fire. From this room access was gained to the battlements via another curving mural stair set in a window embrasure.

The third floor almost certainly dates to the same time period as when the keep ceilings were raised. This room, built on the original castle battlements, which seem to have been removed, has three splayed windows, a fine fireplace and a garderobe set in the thickness of the wall. Obviously comfort was high on the builders list of requirements from this alteration. There is no apparent method of reaching any replacement battlements.

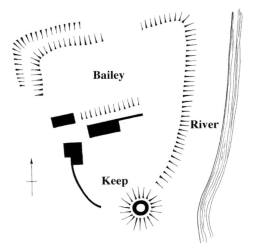

This tower has always been dated to the early part of the 13th century based on supposed architectural styles. However such dating methods are suspect. The story of a fire at the castle in 1165 and the apparent fire-blackened nature of the exterior of the tower, together with its subsequent rebuilding and remodelling, might suggest an earlier provenance. So too might the diagonal tooling which graces much of the better stonework of the castle. The mural stair between the first and second floors is also set on an exposed external front of the castle and its position is quite obvious due to the two rectangular loops that light it. As such it would be vulnerable to 13th century siege engines. The similar method of access to the upper floors at Tretower Castle's keep certainly dates to after 1233, but the stair here was protected by the walls of the shell keep. This may suggest that the initial tower on the rocky outcrop at Bronllys was built by Walter Clifford soon after his arrival in Cantref Selyf in 1144. The change of the roof levels may then date to after the fire of 1165, while later still some of the windows were remodelled and the extra floor added. The argument seems strengthened by the lack of diagonal tooling at Tretower's keep and the superior accommodation and style within the structure. The round keep at New Buckenham Castle in Norfolk was probably also started in the 1140s and there is some evidence that the round towers at Clifford Castle may have been begun before this date by the Tosny family.

The bailey, in which the forebuilding stands, lies east of the keep and shows no traces of ever having been walled. A ditch and rampart, however, are apparent. In this bailey, towards the modern house, is a well and built into the house stables is one end of a wall.

138

This is probably the last trace of a large hall block which was still very visible in Buck's day. The rectangular block in Buck's print appears to have had a parapet, certainly to the north, and a projecting chimney block(?) in the centre of its east wall. At the south-east end of the second floor there appears to be the remnants of a projecting latrine chamber, perhaps similar to that at Longtown Castle, Herefordshire. All the windows and fitments  of the building appear to have been robbed out, even by 1741. The remaining fragment today betrays little of its origin.

Beyond the main bailey was a further large enclosure to the east. The banks and ditches of this still remain, making a large rectangular bailey. It is presumed that both wards were enclosed by palisades. Probably, as Bronllys was a relatively important castle, the wooden defences consisted of towers and gatehouses, some of considerable complexity and similar to those uncovered by excavation at Hen Domen Castle, Montgomery. In the river beneath the castle are the slight remains of a dam of indeterminate date.

Aberllyfni I

Motte and bailey
Location: On the northern edge of Aberllynfi (Three Cocks)
(SO 172 381)
Access: On private ground, but can be seen either from
footpaths to the north-west or south-east

This castle, from an early date, seems to have been appurtenant to Walter Clifford's mesne lordship of Cantref Selyf. The castle was in existence by August 1233 when it was seized by royalist forces, probably under Baldwin Gisnes, when King Henry III was fighting Walter Clifford. It was then granted to Inges the Crossbowman on 29 August. Before 26 September the castle was seized by its erstwhile lord, Hugh Kinnersley, and fortified against the king. Henry Turbeville of Devon was then ordered to retake the castle. Both Hugh and Henry survived any subsequent action and the castle remained in the hands of the Kinnersleys for several generations.

The castle is set on a spur of land projecting into the River Wye flood plain on the north bank of the River Llynfi. The apex of the site is occupied by a small, 3m high motte on which there is stone lying about, suggesting that this was probably once a small round tower, similar in many respects to its compatriot at Pipton. South of the motte/keep is a largely ploughed out bailey. Some 60m beyond this is an outer bailey, again largely ploughed out. South-west of the castle is the site of Aberllyfni's ruined church.

Aberllynfi II

This mound is situated on the bluff of the Wye flood plain just

Mound
Location: On the eastern edge of Aberllynfi (Three Cocks) (SO 175 383)
Access: On private ground next to a footpath

beyond bow shot of Aberllyfni Castle. It consists of a 3m deep ditch which isolates a resultant 'mound' consisting mostly of bedrock overlooking the flood plain. The ditch appears to have been rock cut and as this would have taken some effort it could not have been done by natural agencies as has been suggested. This is fairly obviously a man-made site and it would seem best to judge it as a siege castle of Aberllyfni, perhaps dating to the troubles of 1233.

Crickadarn I

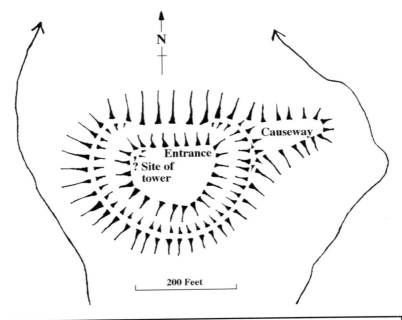

Ringwork
Location: South-west of Crickadarn, itself south-west
of Erwood on the A470 (SO 088 421)
Access: On private ground but can be seen from the footpath
which heads south-west from the church

Little can be said of the history of this site. The grant of this region
to Dore Abbey around 1170 probably indicates that the ringwork
pre-dates this, but the mention of Walter Clifford's land of Clettwr
(the brook which flows through Crickadarn) in 1252 may well
suggest that Walter kept an interest here and possibly also a castle.
Certainly, the disturbances in this region in the 13th century suggest
that a fortress here would have been useful to both the Normans and
the Welsh.

The site of Crickadarn 'Castle' lies in the suggestively named
Castle Field. It consists of a large ridge set in a somewhat marshy

hollow with the Clettwr flowing past less than half a mile to the north. The roughly circular top of this ridge has been scarped and ditched to form an enclosure about 60m in diameter. The ditch is roughly 4m deep around the site and has an additional counterscarp on all sides apart from the north where the fall is slightly greater. This counterscarp is considerably greater to the east, being some 2.5m high from the ditch bottom. As entrance to the site was fairly obviously gained here, it may be presumed that these two facts are related. Around the other two sides the counterscarp it is only some 1m to 2m from the ditch bottom.

In the ringwork ditch there is much rubble which lines the sides and breaks through the ramparts, though no real trace of masonry is anywhere apparent. Neither is there any internal rampart to the ditch as might normally be expected in a ringwork. At the north-western apex of the ward is a rubble mass, some of which appears to be set in a poor mortar, though this may be a natural conglomerate. This slightly raised feature may tentatively be interpreted as a circular tower measuring some 8m in external diameter. If this is so then it may have been the keep. Some form of gatehouse might be expected at the entrance, but other than a slight protrusion towards the causeway and a corresponding increase in rubble on the banks and in the ditches no trace of this can now be seen.

To the east of the ringwork and its entrance is a causeway that runs directly towards the ancient church around which the original settlement of Crickadarn, or Clettwr as it may have been known, seems to have clustered. This long feature ends abruptly with two old oak trees and much river-washed rubble, marking a sudden drop in ground level. It would seem an unlikely shape for a natural feature, yet nothing can be seen that suggests any man-made improvements have been carried out to the causeway.

Crickadarn II or Wuan Gunllwch

Partial ringwork
Location: 2 miles west-south-west of Crickadarn (SO 059 413)
Access: A public footpath passes by the site

The high moorland site of Wuan Gunllwch ringwork is 400m above sea level. As at Twyn y Garth in Radnorshire there is a nearby 'mound' or 'earthwork' marked on OS maps, south-east of the 'castle' at SO 062 412. This consists of a circle of stone rubble about 1.8m thick and 5m in internal diameter, with a break, which may have been the original entrance, to the north-west. This entrance is aligned with that of the castle.

Waun Gunllwch's own 'half ringwork' or 'armchair', as it is described by D.J. Cathcart King in *Castellarium*, is indeed a curious structure, with the spoil from the ditch being used to create a high bank on the exposed eastern side. Aerial photographs emphasise its wild and spectacular position between the headwaters of the Scithwen and Clettwr, whilst on the ground it is best seen from the east. The ringwork ditch to the east is some 10m deep from the barely silted base to the top of the inner rampart. To the west, where the scarp of the hill offers greater protection, the ditch is only some 3m deep and has no internal rampart. Surrounding the ditch on the west side is a weak counterscarp bank, almost entirely removed by rabbits, and correspondingly more prominent to the more vulnerable east. Erosion by farm stock of the counterscarp has unearthed some of the construction material, and it appears that the bank was built in two or three different sessions or periods. At the lowest point, half-way down the ditch, the counterscarp consists of a fine grey clay, above which is a whiter band of clay, which in turn is followed by a reversion to grey clay. On the very top of the bank is much angular rubble, which may indicate masonry defences, perhaps a low mantlet wall on the exposed eastern front. Certainly no trace of masonry has been visible on the less substantial parts of the bank, especially in the rabbit damaged portions where traces might have been expected.

There is little sign of any rubble in the main rampart. This itself is split into two unequal parts by the entrance causeway that fills the

144

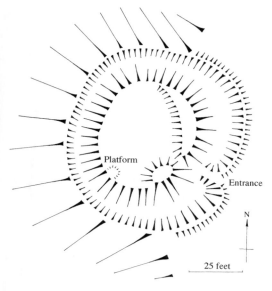

Platform

Entrance

N

25 feet

ditch to the south-east. The rampart itself is steep at the front, but tails off gently into the interior. The internal platform is roughly level although a slight south to north and east to west incline is apparent. On the west, where there is no rampart, several features are apparent on the ground. At one point there is a slightly sunken square platform about 3m across. To the east of the paltform is what might just be the rubble remains of the foundations of a curtain, or more likely mantlet wall, about 1m thick. To the north of the platform is what may have been a robber or foundation trench which ran around the lip of the ring-work towards the rampart. If this is a robber trench then it may suggest a thorough demolition of the site; but if it is a foundation trench then it is more likely that the castle was never completed.

Assuming that Wuan Gunllwch actually was a castle, then who would want to build this splendidly isolated castle and why? Its positioning towards the western extremity of the land of Llaneglwys could suggest that it was built by a Clifford, and as such it would seem that Walter Clifford (d.1190) was the most likely builder, though the possibility that it is a reaction hy his son or grandson to the power of Gwynedd in the first half of the 13th century cannot be ignored. Alternatively the castle might have been the work of Llywelyn Fawr, whose men under Madog Fychan of Llangynog had an interest in this area. Similarly, as late as 1245 Prince Dafydd and Rhys ap Maredudd of Dryslwyn seem to have been actively pursuing their rights in this district.

Llyswen

'Motte'
Location: On the south-west edge of Llyswen (SO 131 376)
Access: On Private ground between two footpaths west of the village

This 'castle', which has been dismissed by D.J. Cathcart King as a tree ring on a natural hillock, consists of a mound and possible enclosures set on a projecting spur dominating the little village of Llyswen. The mound seems unlikely to be a natural rock outcrop in such a position, and the fact that it has been dug into suggests that it is at least partially soil. It has a surface diameter of 8.5m, is only about 2m higher than the platform to the north, but is more like 8m above the field to the south. No ditching can be determined around the mound at all, although much loose stone is in the 1.7m thick 'rampart' on the 'motte' and in the field boundaries, whose 'ramparts' seem more substantial than mere boundaries. The oak tree which sits powerfully astride the 'motte's' ramparts is at least 400 years old and contains many large, water washed boulders tangled up in its partially exposed roots. It would seem likely that these stones would have had to be manually moved here rather than simply occurring on this rise through some natural agency. During World War II a 'command post' was dug into the top of the mound, according to two local residents. What this work consisted of is now impossible to ascertain, but what is certain is that even a three pounder set here would control the valley and the main road up from Glasbury and Bronllys. The considerations of strategy do not change over the centuries.

The 'bailey' defences are very slight. Beneath the mound to the south is a slight platform some 5m across, terminated by a slight 'rampart' set under an overgrown hedge. This is followed, running south, by a short drop, another platform of about 10m and then a steeper fall into the present metalled road. To the north of the mound lies a gentle slope up to a field boundary which consists of a slight rampart running east to west across the hillside. The eastern front of the area enclosed by this boundary is covered by a deep stream bed running down from the 'hill-fort' above. The western flank is covered by the northern boundary gently curving round to a natural(?) rise in the ground that covers the road and the lower platform. The area covered by this 'work' is undoubtedly too large to be defensive in a castle sense.

Above this supposed castle of Llyswen lies what has been classified as a hill-fort (SO 128379). However the site is built not on a hilltop, but on a quite considerable north to south orientated slope. On the northern up-hill side are powerful twin ramparts with corresponding ditches which fairly obviously once included substantial masonry defences. The other three sides of the roughly rectangular 'fort' show no such substantial works, merely an impressive ditch and slight inner rampart. The downhill side, which appears to have included the roughly central entrance, also had twin ramparts, but these were nothing like as impressive as those guarding the obviously more exposed up-hill side. Modern waterworks have damaged the powerful northern front and made the breaks in this rampart suspect. Most likely none are original. A pond has also been added in the south-west corner of the fort ditch to make use of the natural springs above the site.

Considering the peculiarity of these two sites some interesting speculations can be made. Firstly, it could be that the 'hill-fort' is the site of a Dark Age court from which Llyswen (the White Court) takes its name. Traces of such llys are notoriously difficult to find even when the name apparently survives. Secondly, it may be supposed that the 'castle' lower down the hill is the successor to the 'hill-fort'. If this is so, the large outer defences at the 'castle' may well mark a large courtyard in which a later llys stood when the high-lying earlier defences were abandoned in favour of a more accessible (defensible?) and hospitable site. If this speculation is correct it would suggest that Llyswen was the centre of a now lost commote. As Llyswen is roughly centrally situated in the area of Cantref Selyf granted to Walter Clifford around 1144 this may well be correct. Due to the nature of the Norman conquest of south Wales, most of the old commotal structure has been lost or disfigured beyond credible reconstruction, so such a scenario is not impossible. What we do know of the area is that it was under

Clifford control in the period *c*.1144 to *c*.1170 (Gwenddwr and Nanteglwys to the north and Bronllys to the south) and that this was due to the land being granted to them either by the Hereford lords of Brecon or by the Tosny family (Elfael and Glasbury), both of whom were holding lands in these districts from the earliest days of the Norman conquest of south Wales. Later, this land seems to have been outside the estates granted to Dore Abbey around 1170 and so remained in Clifford hands until the family's extinction in 1263/7. In 1278 Llyswen was being used as a port for transporting materials up the Wye to Builth Wells Castle. It is also not impossible that this region kept its Welsh lords or *uchelwyr*, and that they resided at Llyswen and acknowledged the authority of the Clifford lords of Bronllys and their predecessors of Brecon. As such it is possible that this was a castle of Gruffydd Vaughan, the possible lord of Llangynog and bailiff of Walter Clifford in this district in the 1240s.

Blaenllynfi

Remains of curtain wall and collapsed towers
Location: 2.5 miles north of Llangynidr (SO 145 229)
Access: In woodland on private ground

This centre of the Fitz Herbert Barony of 1208 was probably constructed in the years 1208 to 1215, after which it fell into the hands of the Braose family. It was returned to the fitz Herberts in 1217/8 and was sacked by Prince Llywelyn ab Iorwerth and Richard Marshall in October 1233. Rebuilt soon afterwards, it was apparently taken by Llywelyn ap Gruffydd late in 1262. It was retaken by September 1273 when Reginald fitz Peter fitz Herbert was rebuked for his castle-taking activities in Brecknock. The castle was seized by the Crown after the abortive uprisings of 1321-2 and given to the Dispensers until their overthrow late in 1326. By this time the castle was nearly ruinous and an inquisition of 23 January 1337 held at the castle found numerous defects, which suggests that the castle had never recovered from the attentions of Llywelyn ap Gruffydd, even if the archaeological evidence does suggest that the castle defences were improved at this time.

The inquisition jury found that there was a five-storied tower at the castle called 'Le holestour', which had begun to deteriorate in the time of Reginald fitz Peter (1248-86) and by the time of Hugh Dispenser (1321-26) had become totally ruinous both in its joists and in the roof. These defects could not now be repaired for less than £10, and likewise the weakness in the walls of the castle could not be repaired for less. There had also been a larder built as a lean-to against the curtain wall, but this had fallen down entirely in the time of John fitz Reginald (1286-1310) and could not be repaired in its timber and roofing for less than £3. Next, the 'Knight's Chamber' was examined and was found to have been a one-storied building with a garderobe, which was in such a bad state of repair during the tenure of Hugh Dispenser (1321-26) that the jurors thought that it needed rebuilding in its entirety at a cost of £10. The castle grange, which lay between this chamber and the great tower, had collapsed in the time of John fitz Reginald (1286-1310) and could not be rebuilt for less than 100 marks, likewise the kitchen near the hall, which collapsed between 1321 and 1326, could not be repaired for less than £5. Unfortunately the hall and its adjacent tower which had been in a bad state since the time of Reginald fitz Peter (1248-86) was now so ruinous in its walls and timber that they could not be rebuilt for less than £100. The chamber of the lord and lady and the nursery were likewise found to be ruinous since the

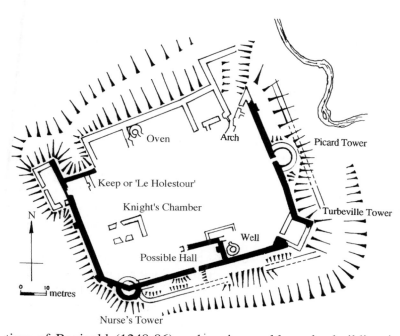

Oven

Arch

Picard Tower

Keep or 'Le Holestour'

Knight's Chamber

Turbeville Tower

N

Well

Possible Hall

0 10 metres

Nurse's Tower

time of Reginald (1248-86) and again would need rebuilding in their entirety for a cost of not less than £100. The larder and granary which was between the Turbeville Tower and the chapel had collapsed between 1321 and 1326 and could not be rebuilt for less than £20. The Turbeville Tower itself was likewise decayed and would cost £100 in repairs. The bakehouse had entirely collapsed in the time of John fitz Reginald (1286-1310), while the brewhouse had collapsed sometime earlier and now they could not be rebuilt for less than £40. The roof of the four-storey high Picard's Tower had collapsed between 1248 and 1286 and this would now cost over 100 marks to repair.

The jurors then turned their attention to the walls and found that 'the defects of the walls of the said castle and the outside walls of the same castle and the tower which is called Nurses Tower, began to deteriorate in the time of Reginald fitz Peter (1248-86)' and could not now be repaired for less than £5. Also the chapel and the wine cellar beneath it and the well were out of repair and so far ruinous that they also required expenditure of £5. Finally, and most interestingly they commented that the leaden water conduit within the castle had begun to deteriorate in the time of Edward II (1307-26) and likewise required £5 of expenditure. Taken together this suggests that Blaenllyfni Castle, commenced as a major stone castle in the reign of King John as a replacement for the inaccessible and inhospitable Castell Dinas as the caput of Peter fitz Herbert's new barony, was ruinous by the end of the Welsh wars in 1283. Even more interesting are the names of the towers—Picard and Turbeville. Were these towers built by the service of these mesne lords of Blaenllyfni barony, or were they merely garrisoned and maintained by those families? Further the castle clearly had a piped water supply possibly from its conception in the reign of John. Finally, it is worth noting that no money seems to have been spent on the repair of the castle and it must have gradually slid into further decay.

The castle ruins today consist of one 2m thick curtain wall with a destroyed strongly projecting plinth. Such a plinth was probably necessary considering the wet nature of the site. This towering piece of curtain wall still stands to wall-walk height and a portion of this can still be made out at the wall's summit. Surrounding the site are also the recently cleared foundations of towers and buildings together with four strongly battered buttresses which stand proudly above the collapsed remains of the mighty curtain they once helped support.

The castle was commenced by ditching a rectangular platform formed from a small knoll and filling the ditch with water by means of a dam to the north of the site. Assuming that the jurors made a tour of the castle starting at the keep it would appear that this five-storey tower lay, reasonably isolated, at the west end of the castle. This rectangular structure was entered via a large building which may have been the larder or one of the chambers mentioned by the jurors. Today nothing remains of this long, narrow tower apart from confused foundations buried under turf and masses of vegetation. The loss of this tall, early-13th century tower keep is to be much regretted.

South of the 'keep' a round tower was added to the multi-chamfered south-west corner of the perimeter. This shows two deeply splayed arrow slits commanding the curtain wall to east and west and adding a vague degree of flanking to the angle, the other wall presumably being covered by the keep. Possibly this was Nurse's Tower as it is attached to the now disappeared outer walls. This tower was probably added in the mid-1250s when similar work was being undertaken at nearby White Castle in Gwent, although it is possible that this was either the work of Llywelyn in the 1260s or of Reginald fitz Peter when he regained the castle in the 1270s.

At the east corner of the castle was another long, rectangular tower, this one being smaller than the keep and apparently contiguous with the curtain wall. This was presumably the Turbeville Tower.

Centrally in the east wall a boldly projecting circular tower was subsequently added, which may be the four-storey Picard Tower. The degree of projection of this tower is unusual, and it should be noted that a similar degree of projection is found at Wilton Castle in Herefordshire, and that this is generally assumed to date from the 15th century! North of this tower, at the angle, was the peculiar gatehouse which in design is more reminiscent of an inturned prehistoric gateway than a 13th century castle! On its western flank was a large square building, which might just also have been the keep. If this was so then the tower names suggested above should all be moved one step clockwise. The kitchens would seem to have been immediately west of this tower where ovens still exist. There is also a straight stair which ran down to the basement of one of these structures. The excavations have proven that the interior of the castle is choked with vegetation and collapsed masonry to a level of at least 3m and that much of the castle is still standing to first floor level, buried in its own debris.

The castle well seems to have been close to the curtain next to the possible hall, while the free standing building close to the west curtain may have been the knight's chamber.

The outer walls ran from the gateway round to the suggested semi-circular Nurse's Tower. Possibly this was an attempt to make the archaic plan of this castle more concentric in design. Overall, this castle is a good pointer to changing military ideas, relying initially on its wide moat, tall walls and two great towers commanding both sides of the fortress, for protection. The castle is far from being a Beaumaris or even a Montgomery!

Castell Dinas

Foundations of a major masonry castle,
together with hill-fort ramparts. The highest castle site in
England and Wales
Location: 3 miles south-east of Talgarth (SO 179 301)
Access: Public footpaths pass to west, north and north-east,
and whilst the castle lies on private ground,
several 'paths' criss-cross this site

Castell Dinas is in many ways the key to the control of Brycheiniog. It lies at the head of the Rhiangoll valley, which like its sister valleys the Grwyne Fechan, Grwyne Fawr and Honddu valleys, slope generally from north to south. But the Rhiangoll has one major advantage as a routeway between north and south Brecknock—its head pass lies at only 330m above sea level as against the 632m, 708m and 554m of its compatriots. From the earliest of times this made the valley the natural routeway between the valleys of the Usk and the Wye. Early habitation here is testified by the remains of long barrows and the pre-historic hill-fort that underlies the ruins of Castell Dinas, 461m above sea level. Their domination of this major routeway was undoubtedly their major function and may also account for the lack of a full-scale castle at nearby Talgarth—Dinas in effect was the castle of Talgarth!

Castell Dinas occupies the bulk of an ovoid enclosure that was once a hill-fort with several banks and ditches. Entrance to this fort seems to have been to the north-east where the remains of a later mural tower still stands, the only real standing remnant of this once great castle (A). The main bailey of the castle is roughly triangular, about 78m north to south by 73m east to west on the south front and about 19m at its northernmost point. To the south of the main ward is the middle bailey which occupies the southern part of the old hill-fort. This, at its extremities, is about 90m east to west by 62 north to south. It is not certain whether the outer enclosure to the far south of the site is part of this hill-fort, possibly an annexe, or the later outer bailey of the castle, though the former seems far more likely. Further earthworks, possibly of the prehistoric era, exist to the north, south and west of the castle and are undoubtedly concerned with the various approaches to the fortress. Two causeways, which are probably medieval, approach the castle gates from the west and another, possibly prehistoric entrance, approaches the castle via Dinas Well from the north-east. A gentle rampway runs up the hillside from the south and this may well be medieval, reflecting the route of the earlier road.

When the castle builders arrived at Dinas, probably in the second half of the 11th century, they found a large irregular hill-fort with double, and towards the north-west, triple rampart and ditch defences, probably with the weaker lobe-shaped annexe to the south. The first act of the builders seems to have been to make a straight cut across the hill-fort from east to west dividing the uneven and sloping enclosure into the upper and middle baileys. They then proceeded to build the masonry defences of the castle within the two baileys they had thus created; no intermediate timber stage appears to have occurred at Castell Dinas, unlike many other sites. The subsequent design of the castle is extraordinary. It consists of a rectangular hall keep, chemise wall (a low wall surrounding a structure), inner bailey, upper bailey, middle bailey, and possibly the outer bailey, most of it built concurrently.

To describe this complex structure it seems best to divide the tour of the castle into its constituent parts, starting with the core of the castle—the keep.

The site of Dinas keep is today marked by the hugh pile of grass covered rubble which overlies the masonry remains of this once proud structure. The mound of debris is about 5m high and seems to indicate a masonry hall keep about 22m by 14m externally. Until recently the wall of this tower, uncovered by an unofficial excavation made before 1950, protruded through the rubble at the south-west corner. Surrounding the ruin of this great tower was a further wall or chemise, which was about 34m by 26m. Again, the tentative excavations of many years ago had uncovered the face of this wall. Unfortunately there is no reliable evidence as to the thickness of the keep walls, but these must have been 2m thick or more if the structure was over two storeys high. Local residents also remember that a window used to be visible in the east wall of the keep.

Together the keep and its chemise formed the heart of the castle and draw immediate comparison with the great Fitz Osbern castle

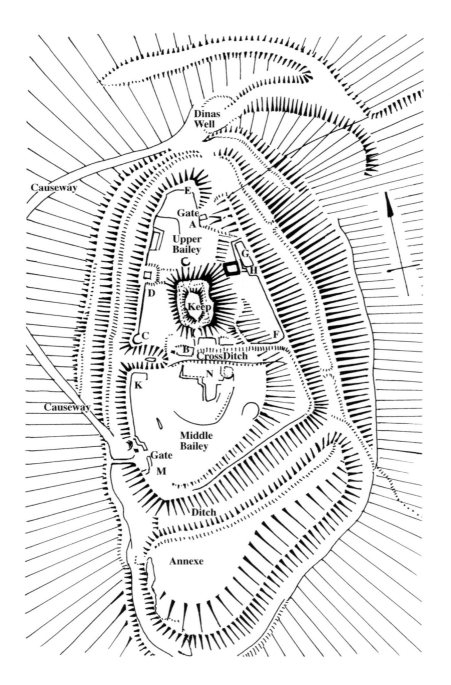

Dinas
Well

Causeway

E

Gate
A

Upper
Bailey
C

G

H

D

Keep

C

F

B

CrossDitch

N

K

Causeway

Middle
Bailey

Gate
M

Ditch

Annexe

at Chepstow where the rectangular hall keep is rather larger at 34m by 14m. Chepstow keep is also built against a strong fall of ground to the River Wye on the west, while Dinas has the steep fall to the east. The keep at Chepstow also had contemporary curtain walls forming baileys to east and west. Dinas likewise has early associated masonry baileys. The comparisons, however, seem greater than this. Similar Fitz Osbern hall keeps of this era have been suggested at Monmouth and Clifford castles. Others may exist amongst the ruins of Wigmore Castle and elsewhere.

The keep commands the upper, northern end of the hill-fort enclosure and particularly dominates the inner ward. Entrance to this ward was gained from both north and south, and no doubt entrance to the keep was also gained from this ward, probably by a forebuilding now hidden amongst the jumbled foundations between the south curtain and the chemise. This would again echo the keep at Chepstow which has an original first floor entrance to the south.

The inner ward was totally enclosed by a strong masonry perimeter, the bulk of its eastern side consisting of the chemise of the hall keep. South of this is a pronounced mound (B) that projects forward into the early cross-ditch. It seems likely that this marks the site of a tower, and though the mound appears circular it would seem likely that any structure it encases was probably rectangular, like the other towers at the site. West of this mound lay a probably rectangular, mainly internal gatehouse which allowed access to the middle bailey. Little of this now remains, but it would appear to have projected some 2m beyond the curtain wall into the ditch and have been some 15m by 8m internally. Due west of the gatehouse are the remains of a square mural corner tower (C) projecting boldly into the ditch to both south and west. Several courses of this tower and the curtain running northwards can be seen from the rubble-filled ditch. This tower is probably still standing to a height of some 7m beneath its shroud of turf and rubble and appears to measure 10m square externally. The rectangular tower at Hay-on-Wye Castle measures 10m by 8m, and as such is directly comparable to the remains of several towers at Castell Dinas. From this tower the curtain wall runs northwards for some 20m to the buried ruins of yet another square tower (D) which is approximately of the same size as that to the south. The main difference with this tower is that it projects internally into the inner ward and northern bailey of the castle, again rather like that at Hay Castle. No doubt it doubled as a watchtower, commanding the northern entrance into the inner ward, the curtain wall of which, which most likely included a gateway, ran from this tower to join the chemise, making the final link in this rectangular ward.

The inner ward is connected directly to the north bailey which occupies the northernmost apex of the castle site and also includes what appears to be the site of the original hill-fort entrance. From the watchtower (D) at the north-western end of the inner ward the curtain wall heads northwards, past the turfed over ruins of a rectangular chamber, for some 20m. It then makes two obtuse angles to reach the northern apex of the castle site. At the first junction there is a slight scarp which goes to form a rectangular enclosure which, after a right-angled turn joins the chemise wall of the keep. Possibly this was some kind of barbican connected with the northern entrance into the inner ward.

At the northern apex of the site is an irregular platform (E) which may mark the site of another watchtower, this one guarding a major entrance to the castle just south of the tower. This entrance pierces the 2.8m thick curtain wall with a roughly 3m wide doorway with jambs for a gate and a timber slot, almost buried, but no trace of a portcullis. The lack of a portcullis would suggest that this is an early feature. Just south of this gateway is another rectangular tower which covers both the gateway and the change in direction of the curtain wall. This tower seems additional to the initial structure as can be judged by its butt junction to the remaining fragments of curtain wall. The rubble-built tower measures 5m by 8m externally and has walls about 2m thick. Its northern half, which bounds the gateway, has almost totally been submerged by the turf, but its southern half is still standing some 2m above ground level. This has had its northern opening blocked by a roughly built wall, possibly to form a shepherd's hut. At some time the buried doorway to the west has also been blocked up. Presuming that this was a ground floor entrance, some 5m of the tower is still standing underneath the turf and rubble that is attempting to suffocate it. The remains of a latrine flue is cut awkwardly into the tower at its south-eastern junction with the older curtain. This shows conclusively that another floor once graced this structure.

At the north-eastern corner of the tower a curtain wall seems to have run directly east forming another peculiar enclosure between this and the main curtain wall which takes off south eastward from the tower's south-western corner. It would seem likely that this tower and one of the associated curtain walls was a part of the refortification of the castle after its destruction by Llywelyn Fawr and Richard Marshall in late October 1233.

The curtain, at the base of a 30 degree slope, makes an obtuse turn and then runs along the scarp of the hill to a right angled junction with the inner ward wall (F). Internally this creates a shelf of land approximately half way between the hill-fort ditch and keep. Its position is peculiar and emphasises the problems with hilltop sites, especially when, as at Dinas, that hilltop is neither regular nor level. The hill-fort ditch parallels the curtain at an approximate distance of 10 to 15 metres below it.

In the enclosure created by the curtain are the foundations of a long rectangular building (G) with a great pit marking a cistern, or more likely a well, at its south western end. South of the building is a rectangular platform (H) which may mark the site of another internal rectangular tower approximately 8m square externally. From here the curtain wall runs southwards for another 35m where another, more triangular, possible tower platform (F) marks the junction of the southern curtain wall. From this 'tower platform' the curtain rises back up the slope towards the keep and the circular mound which probably encases a square tower. This tower (B) would have dominated the line of the curtain with its associated cross-ditch.

South of this main masonry castle defence lay the middle bailey. Like its northern counterparts this seems to have been walled in stone from the first. This view is further emphasised by the junction of the curtain wall of the eastern bailey with that of the south bailey at the triangular 'tower platform' (F). There appears to be no break in continuity as the bailey rampart sweeps on southwards to a 120 degree turn which marks the site of the southern curtain wall along the middle bailey. This curtain, or the rampart that marks the site of it, then makes a series of turns at the south-western corner of the ward. It then swings northwards to what appears to be another rectangular internal gatehouse (M) similar to its compatriot in the inner ward. From this structure, which also appears to have a square tower built into its northern face, the curtain runs back up to the inner ward. Here, just south of the inner ward's ditch, it makes a right-angled turn to the east, possibly marking the site of yet another internal rectangular tower (K). Centrally in the north curtain wall of the middle bailey is a series of large rectangular structures (N) which may mark the site of a later hall block, or even a post-medieval farmhouse. It is not aligned to the inner ward gatehouse and was consequently built when this was obsolete. It does not appear to be a barbican.

The annexe never appears to have been walled in stone, and as most of its surface slopes heavily to the south and east it can have been of little use to the castle garrison of what was already a massive castle.

The surprise of the castle actually lies to the west where there is another stone ward at the base of the hill! This is at the point where the trackway from the south meets the two that serve the western entrances of the castle. This large, approximately 60m by 25m, semi-circular enclosure was fortified by a rampart and ditch. To the north there is much loose stone, and embedded in the rampart is much rubble core of what appears to be a 2m thick curtain wall. This lower defence would really have commanded the road. It might also be the last remnant of a dependant settlement of the castle, long decayed like its ancient protector.

It is virtually impossible to date any castle with a great deal of accuracy, all that can really be done is to suggest plausible chronologies. At Castell Dinas there does not seem to be any doubt that the masonry construction of the castle occurred early in the Norman period. Indeed I would go so far as to suggest that its building would fit easiest into the period of conquest by William fitz Osbern in his campaign in Brycheiniog in the summer of 1070 and expansion by his son in the period 1071 to 1075. The castle would to an extent then have become obsolete with the building of Brecon Castle, the new fortress of Brecknock, in 1093.

As has been suggested above, the remaining standing ruins of the castle, the northern gatetower, probably dates to after October

1233 when the castle was sacked, but soon re-garrisoned. It also seems likely that the great unfinished rock cut ditch on the west side of the castle was made at this time. A similar great ditch was probably begun and never finished at New Radnor Castle, again during this period of emergency. After this flare up of activity the castle would seem to have succumbed to Prince Llywelyn in the winter of 1262-63 when Brecknock was invaded and largely annexed by the Prince. Presumably it was recovered and refortified in the period 1266 to 1274. The castle was surrendered to the king in January 1322 and retained a royal garrison until the return of the Mortimers in 1326. After this the castle, probably already more ruinous than Blainllyfni, was alowed to fall into complete ruin. Leland describes the castle as 'a goode mile from Blaen Leveni [Blaenllyfni] upon the toppe of a notable hille, it is now ruinous almost to the hard ground, there be manifest tokens of three wardes, waulled about...' He goes on to say that the castle was destroyed by the local inhabitants during the reign of Henry IV. Destruction of this Duchy of Lancaster castle by local adherents of Owain Glyndwr seems most likely. In 1741 Buck included a long distance representation of the castle in his view of Bronllys. This shows that the castle has not changed its appearance much in the past 250 years!

Crickhowell

Masonry remains of motte and bailey
Location: Towards southern end of Crickhowell (SO 217 183)
Access: In public park

The castle appears to have been commenced as a motte and bailey, possibly as an outpost of Maescelyn, though this seems unlikely, as they are just a mile apart. However, historically its construction cannot be attested before the 1280s, in which case it may be the youngest motte and bailey castle in Great Britain! The castle was taken by Edward II in 1322 and garrisoned against Glyndwr in 1403. Other than this its military history seems unassuming.

The motte, some 15m high, was at some point in its history fortified with what appears to have been a shell keep whose external dimensions are about 22m north to south by 18m east to west. Entrance to this keep was gained from a twin D-towered gatehouse at the end of a long barbican which descends the motte, probably as one of the bailey wing walls. Only one fragment of one of the towers now stands, three storeys high. Little detail remains of this structure, but there was a first floor fireplace in its thin 1.8m thick north wall. The flue of this exits half way up the wall in a manner reminiscent of the early Norman shell keep flue at Tretower. There is also the slight remnant of a window to the north. On the first

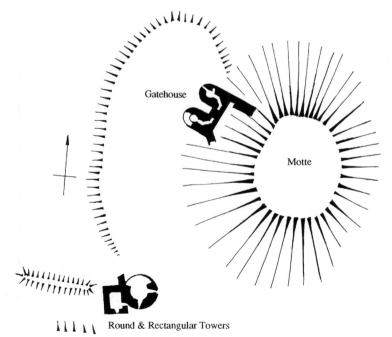

Gatehouse

Motte

Round & Rectangular Towers

floor, half a window embrasure exists to the north together with much plaster. Several corbels and the crease of the destroyed roof above this show that the tower was originally of two storeys and a basement. The remaining part of the window embrasure is similar to those found in the two mural towers described below. Between the two towers lie the remains of what seems to be a drawbridge pit.

To the west of the motte lies the site of the now mostly destroyed bailey. This was once protected by a ditch and possible rampart, and this may again suggest a pre-masonry castle. On the southern side of the motte a wingwall descended to the south-west and no doubt joined up with the main remnant of the castle, a conjoined round and rectangular tower. Both towers stand to wall-walk height, although over half of the rectangular tower and the back of the round tower have now collapsed. The junction of the two structures, though heavily covered in ivy, seems to show that the square tower butts against the drum and therefore is the younger of the two.

The older round tower stands three storeys high and has cusped windows similar to the rebuilding work at Bronllys Castle keep. Judging from the rectangular tower there is probably a buried basement to this tower. Internally the embrasures have similarities to Longtown Castle keep and it therefore seems best to ascribe these features to the late 13th century. There seems to have been a door at second floor level in the tower's west wall. This may have led to a mural passageway or possibly even the wall-walk of the curtain wall. The tower has the slightest of plinths and almost certainly, like its companion tower, 'modern' battlements. At some point in the castle's history this tower has had its western side removed and the boldly projecting rectangular tower built into its structure. This has resulted in the interior of the tower being chamfered off. Two fireplaces now grace this joining wall. These were undoubtedly a beneficial addition to the tower's facilities.

The building of the rectangular tower may not have post-dated the construction of the round tower by many years for it has similar fittings and internal levels. What may be a postern or embrasure is visible in the tower's east basement wall. On the first floor a loop and a window can be traced and two windows appear on the second floor. The third floor has a low loop and as the battlements are obviously modern it is possible that this is re-sited as a 'feature'. That said, this may have been 'servants' quarters' like those found above Georgian and later houses as there was also an embrasure to the south and a doorway to a connecting door between the two towers to the north.

A curtain wall with D-shaped towers and a gatehouse once completed the perimeter as is shown by Buck's print. All that now remains of this is the rampart which may cover the site of the old curtain wall running away to the west from the towers. All of this masonry structure, if built by Grimbald Pauncefot, probably dates to the 1280s.

Garn y Castell

Destroyed ringwork
Location: 3 miles south of Talgarth (SO 158 297)
Access: A public footpath runs alongside the flattenend site

Site of a 'ringwork' castle about 380m above sea level, probably raised by Humphrey Visdelou possibly acting under Fitz Osbern in the period before 1088. The lordship was abandoned to its over-lords, the earls of Hereford and lords of Brecon, before 1144 when the castle site together with the lordship of Penllanafel had been granted to Brecon Priory. It is to be assumed that the castle was then either demolished as part of the gift, or was allowed to decay soon afterwards. This suggests how strong the Normans felt their posi-tion to be in the Talgarth area in the early 12th century.

The 'ringwork' is in a good position on a promontory over-looking the road which runs up through the little farmstead of Penllanafel, once the centre of the lordship of Walekin Visdelou. Little now remains to show that any fortification stood here, but a rise in the field at this point may indicate the site of a ringwork similar to that at Trefecca Fawr. The slight mound is about 30m across and commands the low ground from Llangorse to Trefecca. Behind the site the ground soon rises steeply to the bare slopes of Mynydd Troed.

Hen Castell

Tower foundations
Location: 1 mile south of Crickhowell (SO 213 166)
Access: Visible from the minor road to its south,
and public footpath to its east

The old castle (Hen Castell) of Llangadock is perched on sloping ground on the opposite side of the River Usk to the town of Crickhowell. It has been suggested as a square motte, but more likely it is just the ruins of a square tower house possibly similar to those found at Talgarth and Scethrog, except for the fact that this one definitely had a moat. The site of the castle, from which magnificent views of the hill-fort Crug Hywel can be obtained, is situated on the point of the hillside where the slope is comparatively gentle. The position was undoubtedly chosen for the abundant water supply which bursts from the ground here in several springs. The earthworks of the now mostly emptied moat form a square roughly 25m internally. Inside this are the remains of a rectangular structure about 23m east to west and 16m north to south. To the north the ground slopes, in places quite dramatically down into the damp, marshy moat bottom. Presumably some form of barmikin or wooden structure stood here in ancient times. The walls of the rectangular building seem to be about 2.5m wide and the rough external face of the wall can still be seen at external ground level to the south. This suggests that the entire 'motte' is made up of the soil covered ruins of the tower. Probably it was built by the Turbevilles, before Crickhowell was founded.

Maescelyn

Motte and bailey
Location: 1 mile north-west of Crickhowell (SO 206 195)
Access: On private ground, but readily visible from the adjacent
A40 to its south

The Turbevilles were the first and possibly only owners of Maescelyn Castle. The castle was not mentioned in any campaigns, but we can assume that the district was overrun by both Prince Llywelyns in October 1233 and December 1262. Whether the castle held out is unknown.

Maescelyn Castle is on a site set close against a steep dingle which contains a stream that flows down to the nearby River Usk. To the north and east are meadows that climb steeply up the side of the Black Mountains. The motte, about 3m higher than the bailey platform and 6m above the brook, is distinctly oval, being about 20m north to south by 10m east to west. The northern half of the motte is also distinctly lower than its southern part, due to the southern part having once supported a tower about 10m square. At the south corner of the upper portion of the motte are the internal foundations of a small 2m square room. Possibly this was a corner turret similar to those still seen at Hopton Castle, Shropshire. South and east of the motte lies the damaged remnant of a bailey. Beyond this is said to be the site of St Mary's Chapel, mentioned in 1303 when it is to be presumed the castle still stood. There is a great similarity between the motte here and at Hen Castle, Llangadock, on the other side of Crickhowell. Both should therefore be attributed to the Turbeville family.

Scethrog Tower

Tower remains are incorporated into a private house
Location: South of Scethrog on the A40 (SO 104 248)
Access: Private house, but can be seen from a lay-by on the A40

Probably the centre or caput of the lordship known in the 11th century as Llansantffraed and held by Walter Cropus. By the mid-12th century it had passed into the hands of the Picard family of Tretower. Although not mentioned in any historical account, its history would probably have been identical to that of Tretower, even if by the end of the 12th century it was held by a junior branch of the Picards.

No dating of this structure is currently possible, but its strong similarity to Talgarth Tower should be noted. After 1208 the Picards held their land of the Fitz Herbert's barony of Talgarth or Blaenllyfni as it was otherwise known. The square two-storeyed tower appears to have originally been of three storeys and was protected by water defences drawn from the River Usk on whose flood plain it stands. The walls are about 2m thick and the entrance doorway is on the first floor, about 2m above current ground level. Here, as at Talgarth, there was a straight mural stair that led to the upper floors. The windows of this 12.5m square tower were all replaced, probably around 1500, whilst the first floor doorway suggests a 13th century date for the insertion of this feature. The walls still have a fine batter.

Talgarth Tower

Masonry remains of a tower
Location: Near the centre of Talgarth (SO 155 337)
Access: Can be seen from the outside, but is private,
derelict and dangerous

The vill of Talgarth was one of the oldest possessions of Bernard
Neufmarché and may have been in the possession of his suggested
predecessors, the earls of Hereford. Ordericus Vitallius certainly
speaks of the town as being the capital of the lordship of Brecknock
in the 11th century and later charters repeatedly reinforce its impor-

tance, meaning an early castle might be expected. Unfortunately the structural and historical evidence is rather more obscure. Before 1155 Earl Roger of Hereford made a charter which states that his own demesne castles were Brecon and Hay-on-Wye (both well known castles) as well as Talgarth. This obtuse statement may imply Talgarth was also a demesne castle of the lords of Brecon, or that it differed from the other two. Talgarth seems to have had many mesne tenants and these at an early date included le Brets, Baskervilles, Gunters and Tredustans. The settlement was also on the Roman road between Brecon and Abergavenny and therefore, like Castell Dinas, commanded an important routeway. In 1207/8 Talgarth was separated from Brecon Lordship when King John granted it to Peter fitz Herbert as his portion of the Gloucester inheritance. Peter obviously did not like the accommodation offered by his castle at Dinas and possibly the tower in Talgarth itself, and consequently began a new castle at Blaenllyfni. However his third of the barony was initially known as the lordship of Talgarth, and only latterly Blaenllyfni. In 1282 Reginald fitz Peter was holding his court at least twice a year in Talgarth town and it would seem likely that this was held on the upper floor of Talgarth Tower. How old this tower was at this date is another question. The remaining square tower at Hay-on-Wye Castle is stated by some authorities as being as old as the 11th century, and architecturally that of Talgarth could date from the same period. On 2 July 1306 Rhys ap Hywel was enfeoffed with 4 carucates of land at Talgarth at £5 rent by John fitz Reginald and by 1322 Talgarth was formally treated as having a castle. The age of the masonry structure remains debateable.

In the 1530s Leland commented that 'In the English Talegart is no notable building, but a little prison, by Talegarth church, in the town.' This prison has always been assumed to have been Talgarth Tower, however the description might well refer to Tower Farm some 100 yards north of the church. In 1741 Buck's print of Bronllys Castle clearly shows Talgarth church and town in the background. Immediately north and east of the church tower stands what may be a 'pele tower' structure. This does not appear to be the Tower usually associated with Talgarth Castle which stands west of the church above the little River Enig.

The 'castle' consists of a three storey tower, about 10m square with walls at least 2m thick, guarding the bridge over the river at one end of Talgarth market place. Its tactical position at a river crossing suggests an early date and a lordly influence in its building. The basement is entered via a flight of stairs set in the north wall of the tower. This basement, now below current ground level on all sides except the southern, river side, was roughly rectangular and has had a doorway cut through the masonry to lead into a more modern additional building. A fireplace or oven is said to have been in the south wall next to this opening, but the amount of rubbish in this room now hides any such structure. The ground floor of the tower appears to have been entered from the market place to the north, although this opening has subsequently been recut. Above this 'doorway' is a medieval defensive machicolation which strengthens the opinion that this was the original entrance. The two doorways to the south into the other additional building appear to be relatively modern. The entrance in the east wall appears to be of some antiquity. No original lighting is apparent on this floor.

The first floor was reached by a straight mural stairway. At the top of this stair a recent doorway has been made into the northern addition and opposite this in the south wall is another such doorway into the southern addition. Opposite the stairway is a garderobe chamber and small light. Next to it is a deeply splayed window embrasure with stone seats of a typical medieval variety. Two corbels can also be seen on this floor. The next floor is reached from a dog-legged mural stair starting in the eastern window embrasure. This gives access, opposite a small light, to the second floor. This large room has a single light to the east and a latrine off the embrasure to the west. The latrine was once a projecting structure and draws comparison with the fine similar construction at Longtown Castle keep which may, with some exactitude, be dated to 1216-28. The stairs continue from the doorway up to the now blocked off parapet which once crowned the tower. The tower appears to have been heated from fireplaces in the south wall, their place now being occupied by modern fireplaces. The reworked pyramidal roof probably dates to within a century of 1700.

Tredustan or Turstenton

Motte
Location: 1.5 miles south-west of Talgarth (SO 140 324)
Access: Private, but visible from the lane behind the farmyard

The name of the castle appears to mean the village or tref of Dustan. Presumably he was also the castle builder. All that now remains is a mutilated motte standing some 6m high behind a farmyard to its west. This may overlie any possible bailey. The yard has cut into the motte, destroying its western half; currently it is about 16m in base diameter, but it may originally have been much larger. The motte top is now uneven, but shows no sign of masonry. A field, sloping away to the north, may have supported a bailey, but any trace of this or a ditch around the motte has now gone.

Trefecca

Motte and bailey
Location: (SO 142 323)
Access: It lies behind a bungalow and is not visible from the public bridleway which passes to its south

Trefecca, possibly the village of Vecca or Fecca, stands on the other side of the deep dingle of the Llyfni from Tredustan Castle. The motte and bailey stands between two gulleys cut by a small pair of streams and is therefore naturally protected on all sides except the south-east. Here there are traces of a bailey bank. In common with many other castles the motte stood at the apex of the site overlooking a river, except that here the railway which ran underneath seems to have led to the destruction of the bulk of the structure. What is left is a little under 3m high and 6m in diameter.

Trefecca Fawr

Masonry ringwork
Location: (SO 145 314)
Access: In private land above Trefecca House

Trefecca Fawr ringwork was probably built before the 1080s and stands in a remarkably similar position to the castle of Penllanafel or Garn y Castell. It consists of a ringwork some 27m in diameter, the platform seemingly the same height as the exterior. The ringbank consists of much rubble and stands about a metre high internally, whilst externally the bank is surrounded by a 0.6m deep ditch. To the west the site has been dug into by quarrying, while a barn has been built some 6m south of the ring. The ringbank is the remnant of a stone curtain wall which would have made the castle into a small enclosure, little larger than a shell keep, but lacking the motte, or apparently even the bailey. The name it is sometimes given of Weynard's Castle suggests that the building was English built and it was probably still capable of defence in 1144. However, the survival of this fortress after 1176, by which time all the surrounding land had been granted to Brecon Priory, seems most unlikely.

Probably it was replaced by Trefecca Fawr hall, the fishpools of which could have been mentioned in the later charters of the Baskervilles who held this district.

Tretower

Major stone castle
Location: On the south-west of Tretower (SO 184 212)
Access: In care of CADW and open to the public

Tretower Castle may have been commenced before 1081 when King Caradog ap Gruffydd, the prince of Ystrad Yw, and his Norman followers were overwhelmed by Rhys ap Tewdwr near St David's. It was almost certainly in existence by 1103 and held by Picard, the first baron of that name. Before 29 October 1233 Richard Marshall of Pembroke, then in rebellion, had taken the castle and 'thrown it to the ground'. As a consequence, Roger Picard probably commenced a refortification programme which included the building of the great round tower within the recently ruined shell keep together with the bailey and its gatehouse. It was probably shortly after this that he made a grant to St John's Priory of a parcel of land south of the town square beyond the east gate of his castle which was then known as the Boket, or dog-legged gate. In 1245 Roger Picard was granted six great oaks. This, it has been suggested, may have been connected with the completion of the round tower keep. However, as war was then raging in Brecknock this was just as likely for the repair or building of additional wooden defences at the castle. The defence of the castle was

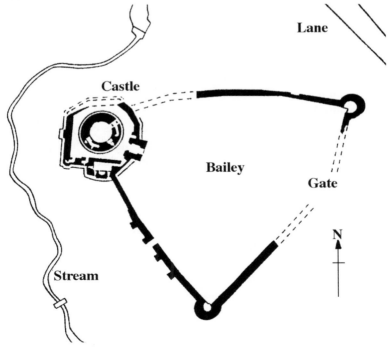

successful in 1245, but the district, then held by Roger the son of the above Roger Picard, swore homage to Prince Llywelyn in December 1262. Despite this act of treason to King Henry III and Roger's subsequent support of the reformist barons under Earl Simon Montfort of Leicester there is no mention of the castle changing hands and it was definitely held by Roger in 1273 even though he had 'adhered to Llywelyn'.

In 1308 the family of Picard of Tretower died out and the castle and lordship passed to the Bluets of Raglan, who seem to have begun Tretower Court as a manor house. In September 1403, their descendant, James Berkeley, was ordered to munition the ruined castle against Glyndwr and this he seems to have done by building a wooden storehouse between the ruined walls of the great tower and the shell keep. With the repression of the revolt in the Marches the castle was no doubt allowed to continue its long process of decay and when Leland passed he mentioned the court, but not the castle.

When the first Picard, or his predecessor, arrived in Ystrad Yw Uchaf he seems to have built a low, revetted mound about 3m high, with a base diameter of about 30m, as his first castle at Tretower. In doing this he ignored the previous Roman fortification at nearby Pen y Gaer and the civil and religious settlement at Cwmdu. His low motte was then surrounded by a 10m wide ditch filled with water from the surrounding brooks that fed into the Rhiangol. This early reveting can still be seen underneath and in places encased by the later masonry of the shell keep. Whether this early knight also constructed a wooden bailey is debateable, but if he did it probably underlies the present masonry bailey remains which are about 60m north to south by 50m long.

Probably during the Anarchy (1135-54), Roger Picard succeeded his father and also acquired the nearby lordship of Llansantffraed which was later to be known as Scethrog. Roger probably used his enhanced wealth to build the ornate shell keep in his massively expanded lordship. This new fortification consisted of a curtain wall some 10m high and a square gatehouse to the east. This new keep used the thin revetment of the earlier motte as its batter and had walls just under 2m thick. Such thinness is probably indicative of an early date.

The shell keep seems to have initially consisted of a residential block running east to west on the south side of the motte. This side also had a five-sided projection which seems to have always housed the castle kitchen. The fireplace in the kitchen with its ingenious smoke dispersal system is well worth a look. On the west wall of the shell was built a long solar range, the motte being lengthened and straightened to carry it. From the north end of the solar range the shell wall ran in five uneven segments to the once tall, squarish gatetower that in the days of Buck still dominated the castle site. The gatetower lay next to the hall block. It is worth noting the

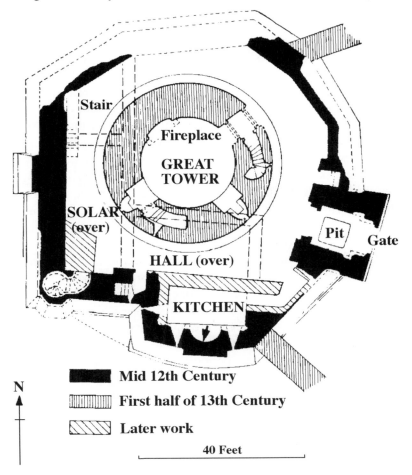

Mid 12th Century

First half of 13th Century

Later work

40 Feet

N

quality of the now blocked windows and doorways which once graced the castle buildings. Buck's print of 1741 shows the shell still standing to its full height, with the battlements apparently rising to the taller north solar side of the keep. All of this wall and the square gatetower have now collapsed.

After the castle's destruction in October 1233 the shell keep seems to have been gutted and the new round tower, perhaps based on that at Bronllys, begun. The original tower seems to have been intended to have consisted of a basement with two storeys above. This was later altered when a further storey was added. Externally the round tower had a sloping plinth and a moulded string course girding its 3m thick walls. Entrance was initially gained to the round tower via a first floor doorway reached by a wooden fore-building of which the steeply pitched roof crease can still be seen. A similar arrangement was used at Bronllys Castle keep, at Skenfrith in Gwent as well as at Longtown in Herefordshire. It should be noted that there was a chamber in the wall of the shell keep opposite the entrance to the round tower and that this may have been part of the access to the inner keep. In the thickness of the wall between the two doors of the inner keep is a mural stairway which leads sharply upwards to a spiral stair which gave access to the upper floors. In the window opposite the entrance is a mural stair that curves down to the basement. Such an access is rather unusual, entry to keep basements is generally thought to have been via an internal wooden staircase. The holes for joists are very apparent between the various tower levels and to the north on the second storey is a doorway that gave access to the shell keep wall walk, probably via a wooden bridge or passageway. A similar arrangement can be seen at Freteval Castle west of Paris, where a round tower within a shell keep are linked in a similar manner at a high level. The roof and rafters associated with this door can be seen to date from a different period in construction as they overlay and cut into the relieving arch and cut stone of the doorway. Probably this was the wooden structure built by James Berkeley in his munitioning of the castle in the early 15th century.

Work on the third floor of the round tower seems to have come to an abrupt halt as is seen by the offset just above shell keep level. This offset has cut through a loop in the spiral stair to the east. The lower part now makes a fine rectangular loop and is topped by the coursing layer. Above it the opening is made into a round headed window! Perhaps the gift of wood to Roger Picard in 1245 marked the completion of this tower after a ten year hiatus in its building. Judging from Buck's print yet another storey stood upon this before the battlements were reached. No trace of this storey or the battlements now remain.

To the east of the shell keep lies the crumbling remnant of the bailey defences, probably built in stone at the same time that the round keep was constructed—now occupied by a farmyard. The remains of this coupled with Buck's print suggests that a large drum tower stood at the two extremes of the triangular ward, that to the north still standing in 1741. The buttresses supporting the south wall still largely survive today, but the apparent postern near to the keep does not. The entrance between two buttresses set between this postern and the south tower was probably relatively recent in 1741 and has now been blocked again, the wall here still standing some 2m high. Other parts of the enceinte stand 7m high. Presumably the Boket gate stood to the east in the now destroyed section of the enceinte. Buck's print also seems to show evidence of what may have been a mantlet wall surrounding the keep on the other side of the moat.

Twmpan

Motte
Location: On the south-west of Llangasty-Talyllyn (SO 125 257)
Access: Can be seen from the minor road to its south

This motte stands about half a mile south of the church and is about 4m high and 15m in diameter. There is no trace of any ditch or bailey. Shortly before 1954 a 2m deep pit was cut into the motte top and this revealed that the mound consisted of a loose mass of red sandstone in moderately small slabs, mostly piled on edge. Towards the motte edge, however, was only red sandstone clay. As D.J. Cathcart King commented, this appears to be a reversal of the normal practice of mottes. Perhaps what we have here, as at Pipton and Camlais, is another free standing round tower, buried in the rubble of its own collapse. Whether its provenance is English or Welsh is again debateable.

Builth Wells

Foundations and earthworks of motte and bailey
Location: To the east of the centre of Builth Wells (SO 044 510)
Access: Criss-crossed by public footpaths

If Caer Beris was the first castle founded at Builth by the Braoses,
then Builth Wells Castle was probably founded in 1208 by the
sheriff of Gloucester, before his forces were defeated and forced
back down the Wye. The sheriff returned in 1210 and completed his
aborted foundation of a new castle in Buellt. The castle was later
seized from King John by the Braose brothers in the early summer
of 1215. The king sent men to aid in the castle's further fortification
in 1219 and the castle was besieged by Prince Llywelyn in
September 1223, but relieved soon after by royal troops. In 1229
the castle was given to Llywelyn Fawr by William Braose and
destroyed soon afterwards. On the death of Llywelyn the castle site
was retaken by John Monmouth in 1240/1 who then began its
rebuilding. The castle was repeatedly besieged between 1256 and
its fall on 17 July 1260, when it was once more demolished.

Seventeen years later Edward I ordered it rebuilt as a 'great tower' on the motte, with 'a stone wall with six turrets surrounding the said castle', and a 'drawbridge with 2 large turrets' and stone walls enclosing the inner and outer baileys. The majority of the building stone came from local quarries, but some better stone for the quoins and fittings came from Cusop and Clifford in Herefordshire, about 20 miles down the River Wye. The lime, which is sometimes stated erroneously to have been unused or under-used in central Welsh castles, was brought from Talgarth, Llyswen, where it had presumably been brought up the Wye by boat, Hay-on-Wye and Radnor. It was then carried to the castle works via ox-drawn wagon trains.

Between 1277 and 1282 £1,666 9s 5$^{1}/_{4}$d, a considerable sum, was spent on building this fortress. However that was £167 10s 6$^{1}/_{4}$d less than the revenue that can be shown to have been sent to the castle, which explains the audit demanded by the barons of the Exchequer concerning its building. Probably in 1283, as a result of this discrepancy, an audit was made of the monies spent between 16 March and 1 November 1282 under the jurisdiction of Stephen Emille, the keeper of the king's works at Buellt. Amongst other matters this found that Stephen owed £40 4s 11d for expenses in connection with the building. Analysis of the roll on which the debts were recorded provide a good insight into the day to day construction work. The biggest overall payment due was of £4 16s for Master William the mason for his wages 'and other things'. In this section follow a further 19 men who probably made up the mason's workforce, most of their names being local ones, including Clifford, Kington, and Rushdock. These men account for £12 15s 8d. Just above them, in terms of money owed, were the carriers, men like Roger the Welshman, Henry and Robert, carters of Radnor, Henry the bailiff of Hay-on-Wye and Pain Esses and his men who had bought and brought the lime for making the walls of the castle. These 13 men were owed £12 17s 10d in total.

Also listed were the quarrymen who cut the stone for the castle. Again many of these were Marcher men such as Einion Ywn, the men of Llanhamlach, Philip Winforton, Ralph Pembridge, Adam Pipton, Alexander Eardisland, Philip Poitevin and Walter Shobdon, though some were from further afield like Walter the Irishman. These and their fellows each received 3s 4d for 5 weeks' work.

Next came the sand-diggers and mowers, men like Roger Poitevin, Walter Clifford, Reginald Rushdock and Robert Winforton who also received 3s 4d, presumably for a 5 week period. Gilbert the smith received the grand total of 14s for 7 weeks work and other men received divers amounts for unknown work although some were carpenters and carters. Miles received 14s for his crossbows and William Joudrel of Hereford received 40s for iron supplied. At the end of the list came the hodwomen who each received 2s for 4 weeks' work. Presumably male manpower was used for harder work! Some of the names are again enlightening: Johanna, Matilda, Cecilia and Alina all shared the surname of Kington, Gwladys Oxford, Nest Eardisley, Matilda Brampton, Malin the Irishwoman, Gwladys Ddu, Susan Glasbury, Margery Radnor, Eve Talgarth, Eve Cantref Selyf, Matilda Brecon and Gilian Winforton. Presumably many of these were wives or daughters of the men mentioned above. All in all the building of Builth Wells Castle, like so many other undertakings, must have been very much a family affair!

At the end of the audit the barons were no more enlightened as to where the missing money had gone, and although they recorded their disapproval no action seems to have been taken to recover the missing amount!

Whilst the wrangling over the missing money went on, the castle needed manning. In 1277, 9 mounted serjeants and 40 foot soldiers protected the site, though after the surrender of Llywelyn this figure dropped to 4 horsemen and 10 infantry. In the winter of 1294 the besieged garrison consisted of 3 heavy and 3 light horsemen, 20 crossbowmen and 40 archers. The force which came to relieve them — 10 knights, 20 heavy and 40 light horse — had to make 5 attempts before they could break through the attacking force and relieve the castle. After this siege the castle tended to become a muster point, with troops gathering here for foreign service in 1319, 1321, 1334 and 1385. By 1402 it had become part of the command of Lord Richard Grey of Condor and he held it throughout the Glyndwr war. In the Elizabethan era the castle seems to have been dismantled after a particularly bad fire which destroyed much of the town. The white house beneath the castle is said to have been built from its ruins, as indeed much of the town of Builth Wells seems to be.

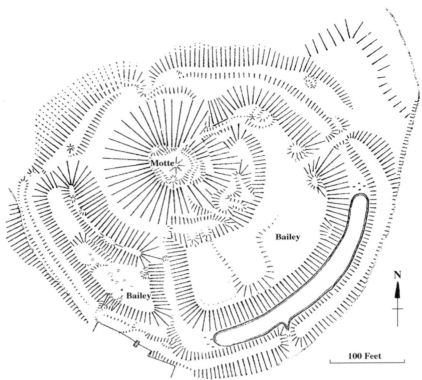

Little now remains of this once major castle except for its earthworks. The castle site lies on a ridge-end site overlooking the modern bridge across the River Wye. It also commands the plain in which stands the ancient church of St Mary's, half-way between Builth Wells Castle and Caer Beris. A circular bank surrounds the whole site and from its counterscarp there is a 10m drop to the valley floor below. The ditch created within this bank was obviously intended to be wet, as it still is to the east, even in summer. Within this circular swimming pool rise three islands that comprise the castle (a motte) and two baileys, each cut off from the other by the moat. The flat bottomed ditches between the counterscarp and the main defences have been drained in recent years by cuts being made in the bank to both north and south. Presumably there must have been springs here before the castle was built. The soil and debris from these great ditches has been thrown up to help create

186

the great motte and the two shallow baileys, a smaller one to the west and the larger one to the south and east. The motte is to the north of the site.

The castle motte is a standard pudding bowl affair, about 10m high from the current moat bottom and 20m across at its summit. A tower keep undoubtedly stood upon this motte, but what its form or dimensions are is difficult to say. If it is 13th century then it would probably have been round or polygonal. However the line of buried masonry on the summit suggests a square tower, though this impression may only be due to the result of ancient quarrying operations. In the ditch south of the motte is a pile of tumbled masonry, which could either be debris from the motte or the main bailey, or the remnants of some kind of barbican to the motte, or yet again even the rubble from the castle piled up ready for removal from the site.

The main or eastern bailey is about 5-6m above the ditch bottom and is connected to the motte top at the north by the remains of a badly collapsed wingwall. There is now no trace of masonry on its surface, although we know from records that at least a curtain wall existed on its outer face. The same is true of the smaller western bailey, but this does have a shield wall on top of its outer face! The purpose of this structure is unknown and its presence quite surprising. Just possibly it is the turfed over remnants of the last remaining part of the bailey wall. However small excavations in it seem to show that it is just built of gravel. Maybe it is a rampart designed to be surmounted by a palisade where the masonry defences were not yet built, and indeed never were.

Caer Beris

Foundations of motte and bailey
Location: In a bend of the River Irfon just to the
south-west of Builth Wells (SO 029 507)
Access: Part of hotel grounds

This castle has for a long time been considered as a mesne castle of
Builth lordship. Yet there is no tenurial history for this and a lack of
evidence of any early knight's fees owed to Builth. The motte and
bailey was probably founded by Philip Braose in or very soon after
1093 when the Normans launched their great invasion and it
became the chief castle of his strictly Welsh lordship of Buellt. It
fell to the forces of Prince Rhys ap Gruffydd in 1168 and was probably never rebuilt.

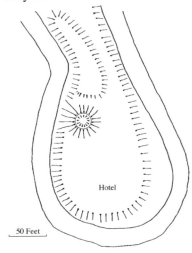

Caer Beris, which seems to
stand for the castle of the
Braoses, was built in a loop of
the River Irfon on a crag of hard
rock which has for centuries
impeded the flow of the river.
The castle now consists of a large
motte standing on a cliff 20m
above the river. The motte itself
is some 7m high and has a
surface diameter of some 20m
north to south and 24m east to
west. The motte effectively
commands the entrance into the
loop and has a hornwork or

bailey to the east and a protected platform some 17m across to the
west. On this platform the Caer Beris Hotel was built at the turn of
the 18th century. The motte top is deeply indented and much rubble
lines the resultant 'ringbank'. It would seem likely that this is the
remnant of either a large round tower, or more likely a small shell
keep. Even now, and as was recounted two centuries ago, there is
much trace of burning on the motte top; whether this is to do with
forestry or the castle's probable fate in 1168 is debateable.

Caerau or **Treflis**

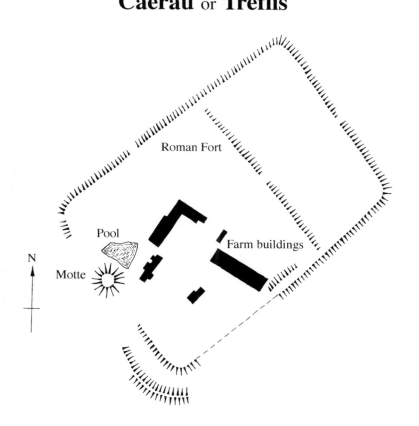

Motte
Location: 1 mile south of Beulah (SN 923 501)
Access: Visible from the road, whilst a footpath passes through
the farmyard in which the motte stands

There is no known history of this castle, but it is possible that it was
once a knight's fee of Buellt Lordship. This 5m high, fine specimen
of a motte stands on the site of a Roman fort. This again may imply
an early foundation date, perhaps in the 1090s. There is no indication that there was ever a bailey, but a large duckpond to the north
and west of the motte may disguise a moat and the Roman fort may
once have doubled as the castle ward.

Llanafan-fawr

Ringwork
Location: 5 miles north-west of Builth Wells (SN 966 557)
Access: On private ground, visible from the Red Lion Public
House, reputed to be the oldest inn in Wales

A moderately sized, double-ditched ringwork lies on sloping
ground west of the church. This may have been a mesne castle of
Buellt Lordship, though it has no recorded history. On 12
November 1259, the church of Lanavanvaur in Buellt had a rector
called Hugh. Whether the ringwork was occupied then or not is
unknown.

In the cantref of Buellt, apart from the major castles at Builth
Wells, there are only diminutive earthworks to mark probably
medieval fortifications. This may suggest that they are all Welsh
built, except perhaps for Caerau, which is of a more standard
'Norman' form. Whether these castles date to the age of the first
Braoses, 1093 to 1168, the age of the Princes, 1168 to 1246 or to
royal initiatives, it is probably impossible to say without a great
deal of excavation work.

Llysdinam

Ringwork
Location: Half a mile west of Newbridge-on-Wye (SN 998 584)
Access: On private ground, visible from the road to its north

The half ringwork at Llysdinam crowns a narrow ridge some 300m
above sea level. This small, weak work, about 13m in diameter, is
defended by a 2m high rampart and 1m deep ditch. The south side
is protected by a 3m drop down a stony crag. Entrance appears to
have been from the west and the defences are strongest to the east,
not surprisingly the side of the weakest natural defence.

Forest Twdin

Small ringwork
Location: Half a mile north of Beulah (SN 919 520)
Access: On private ground

This is perhaps the most curious of all the sites in Brecknock. It is built on a hill 300m high and a great deal of effort has obviously gone into fortifying this 'castle'. Yet it is only 8m east to west by 4m north to south, and as G.T. Clark has commented in *Medieval Military Architecture* it was only big enough to house a wigwam. Outside the 'ringwork' is a narrow horseshoe-shaped, 1m wide, rock cut moat, still full of water. The western side of the castle is protected by the steep fall of the hill. Who built this diminutive castle and why is unanswerable, but the suggestions listed under Llanafan-fawr Castle are as pertinent to this site as to the other minor castles in Buellt.

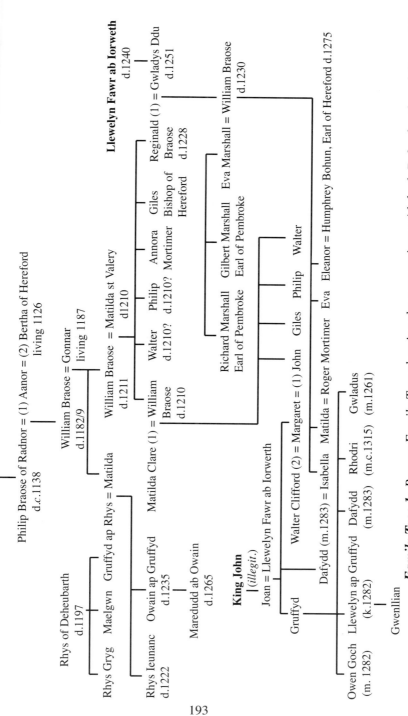

Family Tree 1: *Braose Family Tree showing the connections with both Deheubarth and Gwynedd*

193

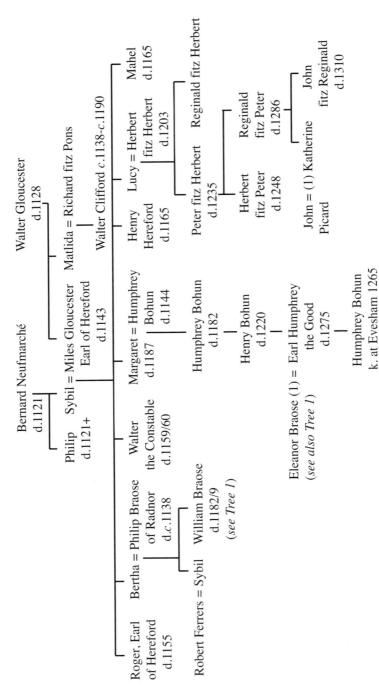

Family Tree 2 *showing the connections between Bernard Neufmarché,
the Gloucesters, Braoses, Bohuns and fitz Herberts*

Also from Logaston Press

Other titles in the Monuments in the Landscape series

Vol. II Castles & Moated Sites of Herefordshire
by Ron Shoesmith. 256pp with some 65 photographs,
plans and maps. £9.95
ISBN 1 873827 59 8

Herefordshire is a county of castles and moated sites, reflecting its position as a well populated agricultural county bordering disputed territory. The history of defence within the county is explained, as is that of castle building, their use and, finally, demise. There is a comprehensive gazetteer of all the sites set out parish by parish with much recent information.

Vol. III Castles of Radnorshire
by Paul Remfry. 160pp with some 35 photographs,
plans and maps. £7.95
ISBN 1 873827 54 7

The history of the centuries of warfare and changing alliances in Radnorshire is covered in some detail for it provides the background to the construction of the castles; indeed, much of the recorded history is about the sieges and capture of castles. Detailed information is also given about all the castle sites.

Vol. IV Prehistoric Sites of Monmouthshire
by George Children and George Nash. 144pp with 40 photographs,
plans and maps. £7.95
ISBN 1 873827 49 0

The authors have developed a picture of human life gradually developing in prehistoric times, from a combination of archaeology and anthropology. Monmouthshire contains interesting Stone Age finds along the shores of the Severn Estuary, in addition to Bronze Age complexes, standing stones and later hillforts. Many of these are detailed in the gazetteer.

Also from Logaston Press

The High Summits of Wales—
A Guide to Walking the Welsh Hewitts
by Graham Uney   £14.95
356pp, 80 black and white and 30 colour illustrations, 20 maps
ISBN 1 873827 65 2

Hewitts (**H**ills of **E**ngland, **W**ales & **I**reland above **T**wo **T**housand feet, with a minimum drop of 100 feet between it and the next peak) are dispersed around a wide part of Wales. Whilst many lie in Snowdonia National Park, (in Gwynedd, Conwy and northern Powys), others stretch eastwards towards the English border at Oswestry, southwards through Cadair Idris, the Dovey Hills and Plynlimon into the wilds of central Wales and the Cwmdeuddwr Hills above the Elan Valley. To their east lie yet more in Radnor Forest, whilst further south a band runs from the English border at Hay-on-Wye westwards through the Black Mountains, Brecon Beacons, Forest Fawr and Mynydd Du above the valleys of south Wales and out towards Swansea. In all there are 137 Welsh Hewitts.

But this book is not just about those individual Hewitts, more the ranges of hills in which they lie. Graham Uney is a qualified Mountain Walking Instructor and his aim is to encourage people to enjoy the different atmosphere of each group of hills

Even a dedicated hillwalker is likely to be stirred by the warmth that Graham feels for the hills, for Part One provides each of the 20 groups of hills with its own section, detailing scenery, routes, stories, atmosphere, bases for exploration and much besides.

However, the book also raises the prospect of 'bagging' the Hewitts, as a counterbalance to the lure of the Munros in Scotland. Part Two tells the story of Graham's own successful attempt to climb them all in one walk in the soggy summer of 1998, when battle was joined with the elements and the hills furthered their individual character.

The Appendices provide a tick list for recording your own 'bagging', as well as information on navigation, equipment and safety, on maps and a useful bibliography and addresses.